Exploring

Macroeconomics

Gross Domestic Product

Long-run Growth

Labor Market

Interest Rates

Inflation and Deflation

Business Cycles

Monetary Policy

Fiscal Policy

Notes and Class Exercises

Instructor: Dr. Jared A. Pincin
The King's College, NYC

Printed by Kindle Direct Publishing, in the United States of America

First printing 2019
Revised 2020 and 2021

ASIN: 1657260585 (Paperback)

Dear Student,

Welcome to ECO 210, Macroeconomics, at the King's College in New York City. This course is an introduction to macroeconomic theory and analysis, focusing on aggregate economic relationships. While mainly a theory course, the course will highlight certain public policies so students may see the intersection between economic theory and the real world.

This booklet contains the notes and class exercises for the course and should make note taking easier so the student can listen more intently to the lectures. The booklet contains all the information from the PowerPoint slides, including graphs, from each class. Since research suggests taking notes by hands increases retention, this booklet provides spots for students to complete during each lecture.[1] Students should also take additional notes beyond the blank spots since the professor will provide additional detail regarding each topic.

This course demands moving beyond memorization of economic concepts and students will need to explain the why's of a concept as well as the what's. I will test to see if students can connect and integrate the material. For example, take the following question. *True, false, or uncertain. The unemployment level is rising if the unemployment rate is rising. Explain.* For this question, the student must understand why the unemployment rate changes, not just what unemployment is.

If you notice any errors in this packet, please inform me so I may correct the mistakes for future semesters. All errors are my responsibility. I hope you enjoy the course and will pursue further studies in economics. Blessings.

---

[1] Mueller and Oppenheimer (2014).

Tips to Do Well in the Course

There is no shortcut, silver bullet, or secret sauce to do well in the course. The best recipe for success is hard work and persistence. However, here are a few suggestions for each student as you navigate the course.

1. **Read the syllabus.** The student can find the answer to most non-material questions on the syllabus. Among other information, the syllabus includes information about assignments, course expectations, the course schedule, and office hours.

2. **Complete and submit all assignments.** Forfeiting points is an unwise strategy for success.

3. **Study from the outside-in.** As you study, start with the big picture and work your way to the smaller details. This will help you contextualize individual lectures and connect ideas throughout the course. Only when you can explain a concept in your own words, and with graphs and math where appropriate, do you understand the concept.

4. **Memorize each definition.** Part of learning any discipline is learning the terminology of the discipline. Therefore, understanding the terminology is crucial to grasping the material in the course. Problem sets and exams have questions where using the definition helps provide a fuller answer. Once I give a definition, I assume you know it for future lectures.

5. **Start early on your problem sets.** Students typically have a few days to complete a problem set. Still, it is common for students to wait until a few minutes before the assignment is due to complete problem sets This behavior harms students and is a poor preparation habit for exams.

6. **Systematically approach the problem sets.** First, try the problem sets without your notes. This way you see what you do not know. Second, try the problem sets with your notes. Lastly, work with others on the problem sets. However, *you must submit your own work and I take plagiarism seriously, even on problem sets.* This is particularly important for the economic reasoning questions. Your reasoning must be your own.

7. **Practice computation questions.** Computation questions are mathematical representations of the verbal theory. Each exam has computation questions that look like computation questions on the class exercises and problem sets. A student should earn a perfect or near perfect score on the computation section of an exam because the technique to answer these questions is the same on class exercises, problem sets, and exams. The math for computation questions is basic arithmetic and simple algebra. *I mean these to be easy points and the grade often shows effort, not ability.*

8. **Put all your computation answers in the correct unit**. $10, 10%, 10 units, and 10 might all have 10 in the answer, but they have different meanings. These meanings matter and a student will lose points for incorrect units.

9. **Approach each graph step by step**. First, properly label the graph (all curves and axes). Second, locate the original equilibrium. Third, determine what curve(s) changes and in what direction. Fourth, after you shift your curve(s), locate the new equilibrium. Graphs are a visual representation of the verbal theory and are common in the course.

10. **Understand how to answer the true/false/uncertain questions**. A question is true if it is true in all circumstances, false if it is false in all circumstances, and uncertain if it is true in some circumstances and false in others. Locating key words in a question is crucial. Some of this is terminology (e.g., nominal interest rate) and some of this is key words (e.g., must). An answer cannot be uncertain with the key words of all, must, or never. *The reason for why a question is uncertain is never because "the question does not contain enough information."* For an answer of uncertain, you must explain why the question is true in some circumstances and false in others.

11. **Provide complete answers for economic reasoning questions.** Do not waste your time repeating the question in your answer. Fully answering a question may require explaining several reasons so provide the different reasons if needed. I can only grade what you write so be clear and specific.

12. **Do not wait to ask for help from the instructor.** The material builds upon itself throughout the semester so waiting to ask questions is an unwise strategy. Take advantage of available office hours and possible review sessions. While I monitor the grades closely and may contact you on my own, only you know if you are struggling because of laziness or because you do not understand the material. Waiting until right before an exam is often too late. I care about your performance in the course but cannot assist you if you do not ask. Remember, the two variables you control are your attitude and effort.

<u>Topic One: What is Macroeconomics</u>

I. Introduction

    A. Definition

        1. the study of movements, trends, and economic relationships in the economy as

    a _____

    B. Three Reasons to Study Macroeconomics and not just Microeconomics

        1. the fallacy of _____

            a. definition

                i. the error of assuming what is true at the micro level must be true

                at the macro level

            b. example related to macroeconomics

                i. relative prices are not the same as aggregate prices so if the price

                of one good rises, this does not mean all prices are rising

        2. the law of _____ numbers

            a. definition

                i. as the _____ size increases, the mean of the sample

                converges to the mean of the population

            b. this means _____ lessens as the sample size increases so

            trends are more likely to be meaningful

            c. example related to macroeconomics

                i. one month of economic contraction does not mean a recession

        3. Good _____ policy eliminates inefficiency and bad

    microeconomic policy creates inefficiency. However, these effects are typically small. The benefits of good _____ policy are

_____ and the devastation from bad macroeconomic policy is severe.

    a. example related to macroeconomics

        i. taxes can change relative prices, but poor monetary policy can

        lead to hyperinflation

C. Types of Macroeconomic Models

    1. macroeconomists use _____ types of models

    a. models with _____

        i. these models explicitly include rational agents who maximize

        utility (for individuals) and profit (for firms)

        ii. definition of rationality

            1. rationality means individuals pursue their perceived best

            outcome

        iii. definition of utility

            1. the well-being an individual receives from an action

        iv. definition of microfoundations[2]

            1. microfoundations are the foundational principles of

            microeconomic _____ of individual agents that

            support an economic theory or model

    b. _____ models

        i. these models do _____ explicitly include rational, maximizing

        firms and individuals

---

[2] Microfoundations are important because *observed* relationships between aggregate variables depend on *current* macroeconomic policy. If macroeconomic policy changes, the relationship between aggregate variables may change. This is the Lucas Critique (Lucas 1976).

2. this class uses *ad hoc* models to explain the basic definitions and concepts in macroeconomics.

II. Macroeconomic Goals of Every Economy

    A. Three Goals

        1. promote economic _____

            a. _____ growth through higher productivity[3]

        2. increase _____

            a. jobs that add _____ to the economy

        3. keep _____ prices _____

            a. stable prices provide _____ information to economic participants

Topic Two: Gross Domestic Product

I. Introduction

    A. Definition

        1. Gross Domestic Product (GDP) is the _____ value of all _____ goods and services _____ within a _____ within a given _____.

    B. Overview

        1. GDP measures _____ concepts at once

            a. monetary value of _____

                i. caution: Production is _____ the same as productivity!

                Productivity measures the _____ of inputs in making

---

[3] Productivity is obtaining more output from a given level of factors of production. Factors of production are the inputs in the production of goods and services. There are four factors of production: land and natural resources, labor, capital, and entrepreneurship.

output.

b. total _____

c. total _____

2. For the _____ economy, these three are _____

a. Why? _____ comes from _____ and income

comes from _____

C. Breaking Down the Definition

1. Market value

a. Goods and services are valued at _____ prices

i. Why? To provide a _____ comparison between

goods and services

b. Goods and services _____ a market value are _____.

i. examples:

2. GDP only includes _____ goods and services.

a. definition of final goods

i. final goods and services are intended for the final user

b. definition of intermediate goods

i. intermediate goods and services are processed with other goods

or services for sale _____

c. Why are only final goods and services counted?

i. to _____ counting the same product _____ than once

3. Current Year

a. GDP only includes goods and services produced _____ the

current year

        i. Does the sale of pre-owned merchandise count in GDP?

           1. only the _____ value created

    b. GDP is a _____, not a _____.

        i. definition of flow

           1. a measurement over time

        ii. definition of stock

           1. a measurement at one point in time

  4. Location

    a. GDP measures the market value of production that occurs _____ a country's borders, _____ of _____ produces it.

II. Measuring GDP

  A. Gross Versus Net

    1. GDP is a _____ measure of output, not a _____ measure of output

      a. GDP does _____ account for the using of resources that are needed to produce the output

        i. example of fish stocks

  B. Different Ways

    1. The Bureau of Economic Analysis (BEA) estimates GDP in _____ ways.[4]

      a. _____ _____ approach.

      b. _____ approach.

      c. _____ approach.

---

[4] For more detail, see Landefeld, Seskin, and Fraumeni (2008).

2. Will use the expenditure approach in this class

3. The BEA computes GDP by

      a. _____ domestic expenditures

    and then

      b. _____ domestic production

C. The Four Components of GDP $(Y = C + I + G + NX)$ in the Expenditure Approach[5]

    1. _____ (C)

    2. _____ (I)

    3. _____ _____ (G)

    4. _____ _____ (NX)

D. Breaking Down the Components

    1. Consumption (C)

      a. definition of consumption

        i. the total spending of household purchases of _____ goods, _____ goods, and _____

      b. definition of durable good

        i. a good used repeatedly or continuously over a _____ period

          1. e.g. automobiles

      c. definition of nondurable good

        i. a good that is only usable for a _____ period of time

          1. e.g. food

      d. definition of service

---

[5] For more detail, see here: https://www.bea.gov/national/pdf/nipa_primer.pdf.

i. a service is a transaction where no _____ good is

exchanged

1. e.g. financial advice

2. Investment (I)

a. definition of investment

i. The total spending on goods and services that are used to

produce _____ goods and services.

b. Includes spending on

i. all final purchases of _____, _____, and

_____ by businesses.

ii. Change in _____

iii. All new _____

c. investment does _____ mean the purchase of _____

assets like stocks and bonds

3. Government Purchases (G)

a. definition of government purchases

i. The total spending on goods and services purchased by

_____ at all levels.

b. G excludes _____ payments, _____ payments,

and _____.

i. e.g. Social Security

c. definition of government spending

i. government spending is government purchases _____ transfers

d. why are transfers not counted

    i. a transfer _____ one person's spending to increase another person's spending

        1. it's like taking money from one pocket to place in the other pocket

e. two caveats on government purchases

    i. C, I, and NX are measured at market prices whereas G is measured at _____

        1. Why? _____ all government purchases have a market value

            a. how much would the Brooklyn bridge trade for?

    ii. C, I, and NX excludes intermediate goods and services whereas G _____ such intermediate goods and services

        1. e.g. security spending

    iii. Why might these caveats be problematic?

        1. _____ GDP

4. Net Exports (NX)

    a. definition of net exports

        i. NX are _____ minus _____.

    b. definition of exports

        i. exports represent foreign spending on goods and services produced _____

    c. definition of imports

i. imports represent domestic spending on the portions of C, I, and

G produced _____

d. Do imports reduce GDP?[6]

i. Claim: Every item _____ could have been made

_____ to satisfy domestic demand.

ii. Reality: The subtraction of imports is an _____

method to avoid _____ domestic production.

E. Confusing Accounting With Causality

1. the formula Y = C + I + G + NX is an accounting _____

a. definition of accounting identity

i. an equality that must be true by construction

2. do not assume _____ if one of the components change

a. a change in one component on the right-hand side of the identity does

_____ mean output changes by the same amount

b. consider the example of fiscal stimulus

F. Inferring Economic Importance

1. the _____ of individual GDP components does not confer economic

_____

2. Consider _____, which is the _____ component

of GDP. Should _____ prioritize consumption over savings?

a. _____

i. more _____, which means _____

consumption, provides additional resources for investment, which

_____

[6] See Griswold (2011) for more detail.

is needed for long-run economic growth

III. Real versus Nominal GDP

    A. Nominal GDP (NGDP)

        1. changes in _____ and _____ change NGDP

            a. this means NGDP can increase (decrease) if only prices increase

        (decrease), if only production increases (decreases), or both

    B. Real GDP (RGDP)

        1. prices are held constant at a base year so only changes in _____

    change RGDP

IV. Miscellaneous

    A. Why do Economists Care About GDP?

        1. it is the _____ measurement of production

        2. a _____ GDP indicates a _____ material standard of living

        3. a higher real GDP makes paying debt _____ since society is wealthier

    B. GDP Does Not Measure

        1. economic activity outside of _____ markets

        2. _____ or _____

        3. _____

        4. _____ of the environment

        5. _____ of income

        6. _____

Class Exercise: **Real and Nominal GDP**

Year	Prices and Quantities			
	Price of Hot Dogs	Quantity of Hot Dogs	Price of Hamburgers	Quantity of Hamburgers
2018	$1	100	$2	50
2019	$2	150	$3	100
2020	$3	200	$4	150

(1) Using the above data table, calculate Nominal Gross Domestic Product for each year.

(2) Using the above data table, calculate Real Gross Domestic Product for each year. The base year is 2018.

Topic Three: Long-run Economic Growth

I. Introduction

    A. Four Stylized Facts of Economic Growth

        1. every country was once _____ .

        2. present GDP per capita varies _____ among countries

           a. definition of GDP per capita

              i. GDP divided by _____

        3. present GDP per capita growth _____ vary among countries.

4. economic growth is _____ and long-term growth is _____

guaranteed

B. Calculating Economic Growth

1. Growth is calculated as a _____ change

2. Gt = $\dfrac{(Yt-Yt-n)}{Yt-n}$ x 100, where Gt is the growth rate, Yt is the variable of

interest in year *t* and Yt-n is the variable of interest in year *t-n*.

3. Rule of _____

a. definition: an approximation of how long it takes for a variable to

_____ assuming a constant growth rate

b. $\dfrac{70}{X}$, where X is a constant growth rate

c. Example: If GDP per capita grows 2% per annum and starts at $40,000,

in how many years will GDP per capita double?

i. $\dfrac{70}{2}$ = 35 years

Class Exercise: **Economic Growth**

Country	Year	Real GDP Per Capita
Mexico	2017	$19,432
Mexico	2018	$19,887
China	2017	$16,782
China	2018	$18,210
Source: World Development Indicators, World Bank		
PPP adjusted (constant 2011 international dollars)		

(1) Calculate the annual growth rate for Mexico and China. Round to the second decimal.

(2) Assuming the growth rates from (1) stay constant, how many years will it take for GDP per capita to double for each country? Round to the second decimal.

C. Two Types of Growth

    1. _____ growth

        a. definition of catch-up growth

            i. growth from increasing the _____ of factors of production

    2. _____ growth

        a. definition of innovative growth

            i. growth from increasing the _____ of factors of production through increased technology from the development of new ideas

II. Solow Model of Economic Growth

    A. Introduction

        1. the Solow Model shows _____ types of growth

        2. definition: the Solow Model is an economic model that explains the dynamics of _____ economic growth by considering changes in factors of production and productivity through technological change

    B. Set-Up

        1. the model starts with a production function of: $Y = A(K, eL)$

            a. definition of a production function

i. a function showing how _____ become _____

b. in this production function

    i. Y = output

    ii. A = level of technology

    iii. K = physical capital

    iv. eL = human capital

    v. for simplicity, we will hold labor _____ and assume

a production function of the following form

        1. $Y = A\sqrt{K}$, where $A = 1$

        2. the production function _____ as the capital

stock grows

c. definition of technology[7]

    i. society's understanding of production _____

d. value of technology

    i. better technology leads to _____ productivity and

better _____ goods and services

e. definition of capital

    i. capital is a good or non-financial asset used to produce

_____ output

f. definition of physical capital

    i. physical capital is the stock of machinery and structures used in

---

[7] More formally, technology is "the currently known ways of converting resources into outputs desired by the economy" (Griliches 1987) and appears either in disembodied form (such as new blueprints, scientific results, new organizational techniques) or in new products (advances in the design and quality of new vintages of capital goods and intermediate inputs). See http://www.oecd.org/std/productivity-stats/2352458.pdf for more detail.

production

g. value of physical capital

i. more physical capital should lead to more output because it gives

labor more _____ to work with in production

h. definition of human capital

i. human capital is the knowledge and skills workers acquire

through education, training, and experience

i. value of human capital

i. the more _____ labor is, the more valuable human capital

is, leading to higher productivity and more output

2. human and physical capital experience _____ returns

a. definition of diminishing returns

i. total output increases at a _____ rate from an

additional unit of capital, *ceteris paribus*

b. consider the production function of $Y = A\sqrt{K}$

Physical Capital	Output	Marginal Product of Physical Capital
0	0	NA
1	1	1
2	1.41	0.41
3	1.73	0.32
4	2	0.27

3. assume capital _____ at a constant rate

i. for simplicity, assume capital depreciates at 1 percent per year

4. assume society _____ a constant percent of its income

    i. for simplicity, assume society saves 20 percent of its income per year

    ii. what society saves, it _____ in capital accumulation and

    replacing depreciated capital

B. Solow Model in action

    1. if investment is _____ than depreciation, the capital stock _____

    2. if investment is _____ than depreciation, the capital stock _____

    3. The _____ state is where capital depreciation is _____ to

    investment. The capital stock remains the _____.

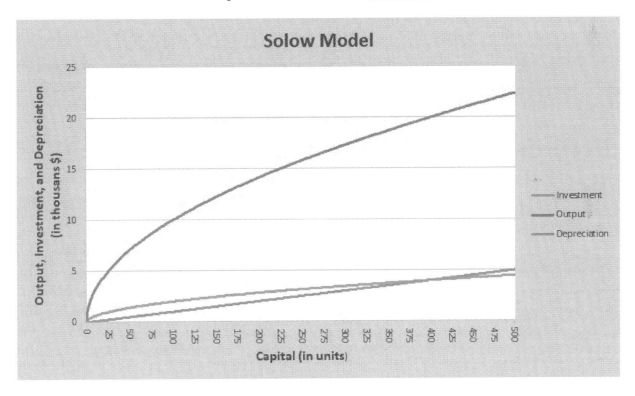

    a. steady state capital stock: _____ units

    b. steady state output: _____

    c. steady state investment: _____

    d. steady state consumption: _____

4. how does an economy grow?

    a. adding more _____ _____ _____

        i. e.g. if a country is relatively poor in physical capital, adding physical capital will create _____ growth

            1. e.g. Germany and Japan post WWII

            2. e.g. China since the late 1970's

        ii. This is true of _____ factors of production. For example, teaching everyone how to read and write yields large gains in output at a relatively low cost compared to everyone trying to earn a graduate degree.

        iii. however, these factors experience _____ returns so growth rates will slow and _____ to a steady state

            1. consider China's recent growth rate

        iv. this is a movement _____ the production function

    b. increasing productivity through _____

        i. this is _____ growth, which comes from ideas

            1. ideas exhibit _____ returns to scale

            2. definition of increasing returns to scale

                a. when the growth in output is _____ than the growth in inputs

5. innovative growth in the Solow Model

    a. let's consider an increase in _____ by 10%

        i. the increase in technology _____ the production and

investment functions _____

ii. new steady states

    1. capital stock: _____ units

    2. output: _____

    3. investment: _____

    4. consumption: _____

iii. an increase in technology increases _____ the steady states

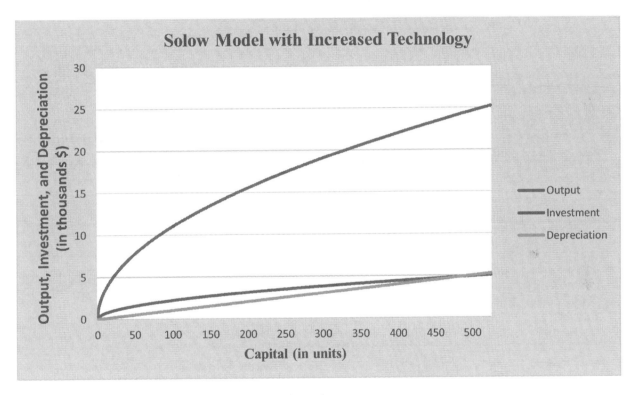

C. Key Takeaways

    1. countries can grow by increasing factors of production

    a. this will _____ cause sustainable growth through time

    2. sustainable growth _____ happens through increased productivity, which

comes from higher levels of technology, which comes from more ideas

D. Digging Deeper

    1. four weaknesses of the model

        a. assumes _____ are given

        b. catch-up growth assumes same _____ for all nations

        c. does not explain where ideas _____

        d. sees population growth as a _____ in the same way depreciation is a negative

    2. why are these weaknesses problematic

        a. institutions are _____ and determine the value of factors of production

            i. e.g. natural resources will remain _____ if people are not rewarded to find and develop them

        b. technology is man-made and needs the correct _____ environment to flourish

        c. people will create and employ new ideas only when they are _____ for doing so

        d. ideas only come from _____

    3. takeaway regarding the weaknesses of the model

        a. institutions are _____ and people are _____, not liabilities

III. Value of Labor and Human Capital

    A. Effects

        1. more labor could affect productivity _____ or _____

2. negative

    a. more labor puts more _____ on resources

        i. e.g. more natural resources consumed

3. positive

    a. more labor allows for more ideas and greater human capital, promoting technological _____

4. economists generally support the _____ case as technology is the only cause of sustainable growth

5. should society worry about _____

    a. _____! The position that overpopulation is a problem is

        i. _____

            1. the Bible consistently affirms life

        ii. _____

            1. we rejoice at births and mourn at funerals

        iii. _____

            1. the only place ideas come from is humans

    b. the near future will show an _____ problem

        i. the world fertility rate is rapidly falling towards the _____ level

IV. Institutions: The Organizing Factor[8]

    A. Introduction

        1. definition of institutions

            a. the _____ of the game (i.e. the constraints on action) that influence

---

[8] See North (1991).

the _____ associated with an action

2. these rules can be _____ or _____

3. institutions are different than policies in that they are more _____

and _____ in scope

B. Institutions in Practice

    1. Aiming institutions (from Principles of Cultural Interpretation)

        a. institutions are _____ and _____

        b. institutions and their practices are pointed at certain _____

        c. institutions _____ us through its _____.

    2. different institutions create different _____

        a. good institutions

            i. reduce the _____ of transaction costs in exchange

            ii. incentivize socially useful behavior by making _____

            others more profitable

            iii. encourage _____ discovery by making it more

            profitable

3. the more _____ and _____ exchange becomes, the

more important institutions are

4. As _____ and the _____ of the market expands, _____

_____ _____ expands, increasing _____. Good

institutions encourage this.

5. Types of good institutions include

        a. Secure _____ property rights.

b. constraints on the _____ class

c. a dependable and impartial _____ system

d. _____ and _____ markets.

C. Growth takeaway

a. Factors of production are a _____ though not a _____

ingredient for growth.

b. Good _____ that encourage cooperation, risk-taking, and the

development of new ideas are needed for sustained long-run growth.

Topic Four: The Labor Market

I. A Biblical View of Work

A. The Threefold Image of God

1. Being made in the *Imago Dei* means we enter three distinct relationships:

a. _____

b. _____

c. the rest of _____.

2. God's first command to humans was the _____ mandate[9]

a. be _____

b. _____

c. _____ the earth

d. _____ the earth

e. _____ over the rest of creation

3. God further explains the mandate to _____ and take care of creation[10]

---

[9] Genesis 1:27-28.
[10] Genesis 2:15.

a. work _____ the Fall

b. work _____ from God making man in His image

c. God commands man to participate in _____ creation

d. our work should honor God and _____ others

e. there is no divide between _____ and _____

II. Labor Market Measures

A. Introduction

1. The Bureau of Labor Statistics (BLS) divides the population into_____

groups[11]

a. Employed[12]

i. definition: _____ employees, _____, unpaid

workers in a _____ business, and those on

_____ leave.

b. Unemployed[13]

i. definition: people _____ working but who have _____

looked for work during the previous _____ weeks and are

currently _____ for work

c. Not in the labor force

i. Neither _____ or _____

B. Four Main Labor Market Variables

1. Labor force

---

[11] For more detail of how the U.S. government measures unemployment, see here:
https://www.bls.gov/cps/cps_htgm.htm#employed.
[12] Each person is only counted once, even if they hold more than one job.
[13] If a person is waiting to be recalled to a job, they do not have to actively look for work.

a. definition: the sum of _____ and _____

persons

2. Labor force participation rate

    a. definition: the percentage of the _____ non-institutional

    adult (16 or older) population in the labor force

    b. Labor force participation rate $= \dfrac{labor\ force}{adult\ population} x\ 100$

3. Employment population ratio

    a. definition: the percentage of the adult population (16 or older) that is

    _____

    b. Employment population ratio $= \dfrac{\#\ of\ employed}{adult\ population} x\ 100$

4. Unemployment rate

    a. definition: the percentage of the _____ _____ that is

    _____

    b. Unemployment rate $= \dfrac{\#\ of\ unemployed}{labor\ force} x\ 100$

    c. caveats about the unemployment rate

        i. it excludes _____ and _____ workers

            1. definition: marginal workers are those who _____ a

            job and have _____ for a job in the last 12 months

            but not the past 4 weeks

            2. definition: discouraged workers are marginal workers

            who are _____ currently looking for work because they

            believe they_____ secure a job

3. marginal and discouraged workers are _____ counted in

the labor force

ii. it does not distinguish between _____ and

_____ work.

iii. it does not distinguish between _____ of jobs

Class Exercise: **Labor Force Statistics**

Scenario: Adult population = 3,200, # employed = 1,600 people, and # unemployed = 200.

(1) What is the size of the labor force?

(2) What is the unemployment rate? Round to the second decimal.

(3) What is the labor-force participation rate? Carry to the second decimal.

(4) What is the employment population ratio?

C. Types of Unemployment

1. there are _____ types of unemployment

a.

b.

c.

d.

2. seasonal unemployment

    a. definition: unemployment due to changes in supply and demand caused

    by seasonal factors like _____ patterns or _____ events such

    as the winter holiday season or summer vacation season

    b. the BLS uses seasonal adjustment to _____ these regular

    fluctuations from labor market data

3. cyclical unemployment

    a. definition: unemployment associated with a _____ in the

    business cycle

    b. this is _____ part of the natural rate of unemployment

4. frictional unemployment

    a. definition: _____ unemployment due to job _____ or

    job _____

    b. it is a result of _____ information in the labor market

    c. it is inevitable because of changing _____ among

    workers and new _____ into the labor force

    d. part of the _____ rate of unemployment

        i. _____ ways to define the natural rate of unemployment

            1. general: the average _____ rate of unemployment

            2. technical: the unemployment rate consistent with a

                _____ rate of inflation (more on this is the

            lecture on business cycles)

5. structural unemployment

a. definition: unemployment due to a _____ between the

demand for labor and the supply of labor caused by a _____ gap, a

change in _____, a mismatch in _____, or too

high of a _____ wage

    i. definition of reservation wage

        1. reservation wage is the _____ wage a

        worker will accept to work

b. part of the _____ rate of unemployment

c. this is a _____ problem that _____ can exasperate

D. The Duration of Unemployment

    1. most spells of unemployment are _____

        a. historically, about 40% of the unemployed are unemployed for

        _____ than 5 weeks

    2. a _____ portion of the unemployed are unemployed long-term

        a. historically, between 15 and 20% of the unemployed are unemployed

        for _____ than 6 months

E. Policy Explaining Structural Unemployment

    1. ultimately, structural unemployment occurs because the given wage is

    _____ than the market clearing wage (i.e. the equilibrium wage)

    2. this can occur for two broad reasons

        a. _____

            i. e.g. minimum wage and occupational licensing laws

        b. reasons _____ to the firm

i. e.g. efficiency wages

3. minimum wage laws

    a. definition of minimum wage

        i. a minimum wage is the _____ wage permitted by law

    b. economists agree a wage _____ high will cause fewer _____,

fewer _____, or both

        i. how high the wage must be is an empirical matter, where there is

        _____

    c. Case Study: Seattle, Washington

        i. In April 2015, the Seattle City Council approved a minimum

        wage of _____ starting January 1, 2017

        ii. the minimum wage will increase in _____ and will

        _____ by _____ of company

        iii by _____, all companies must pay the _____ minimum

        wage

        iv. the results so far show[14]

            1. _____ hours for workers in low-wage jobs, leading

        to a _____ in total earnings

            2. _____ entrants in the labor market

    d. Case Study: Denmark

        i. there is a _____ minimum wage for workers under-

        18 and over-18

            1. the minimum wage _____ 40% when a worker

---

[14] For more detail, see here: https://evans.uw.edu/sites/default/files/webform/w25812_summary_final.pdf.

turns 18

    ii. the results show[15]

        1. employment _____ by one-third and hours

    fall by 45% when workers turn 18

4. occupational licensing laws

    a. definition

        i. laws requiring workers to obtain a government

        _____ to conduct business.

    b. Data[16]

        i. in 1950, _____ percent of US workers needed a license

        ii. today, _____ percent of US workers need a license

    c. Examples

        i. doctors, lawyers, dentists, barbers, florists, and sports announcers

    d. only _____ states allow reciprocal licenses from other states:

    Arizona, Montana, New Jersey, and Pennsylvania

    e. Economic effects[17]

        i. wage _____ for license holders

        ii. _____ employment

        iii. acts as a _____ from consumers to license holders

        iv. may reduce _____ because of fewer service

    providers

        v. pushes least-skilled workers into _____ but more

---

[15] See Kreiner, Reck, and Skov (2019).
[16] See Kleiner and Krueger (2010).
[17] See Kleiner (2000).

_____ jobs

    5. efficiency wages

        a. definition

            i. when firms _____ pay their workers _____

            the market wage

        b. Four reason why firms may pay efficiency wages[18]

            i. improve worker _____

            ii. reduce worker _____

            iii. improve worker _____

            iv. increase worker _____

Topic Five: Price Levels

I. Introduction

    A. Basic Definitions

        1. relative prices

            a. definition: the price of one good in terms of _____ good

        2. aggregate price level

            a. definition: a measurement of the _____ level of prices

        3. inflation

            a. definition: an _____ in the general level of prices

        4. deflation

            a. definition: a _____ in the general level of prices

        5. disinflation

            a. definition: a _____ in the inflation rate

---

[18] See Yellen (1984).

B. The Value of Money

    1. the _____ of goods and services money buys reflects its value

    2. the value of money depends on the _____ price level (P)

        a. $\frac{1}{P}$ is the value of $1

            i. the value of money is _____ related to the price level

        b. example: basket of one candy bar

            i. if P = $2, the value of $1 is _____ candy bar

            ii. if P = $3, the value of $1 is _____ candy bar

II. Change in Aggregate Price Level

    A. Introduction

        1. the U.S. central bank (the FED) evaluates _____ price indices[19]

            a. _____ Price Index (CPI)

            b. GDP _____

            c. Personal _____ Expenditures Price Index (PCEPI)

            d. _____ Price Index (PPI)

        2. The FED explicitly _____ headline PCE inflation[20]

        3. to find the change in the price level, use a standard percentage change formula

            a. $\pi_t = \left(\frac{Xt - Xt-n}{Xt-n}\right) \times 100$

                i. π_t is the change in the aggregate price level in time period t

                ii. Xt is an aggregate price level in time period t

---

[19] For more detail, see here: http://www.federalreserve.gov/faqs/economy_14419.htm.
[20] To be more precise, the FED targets the Personal Consumption Expenditures: Chain-Price Type Index (PCEPI).

iii. Xt-n is an aggregate price level in time period *t-n*

B. The Consumer Price Index (CPI)[21]

    1. definition: measures the cost of a basket of goods and services bought by a

    _____ consumer

    2. the consumer price index is calculated using four steps

        a. _____ the basket

        b. find the _____

        c. compute the basket's _____

        d. chose a _____ year and compute CPI

Class Exercise: **Consumer Price Index**

Suppose the basket is 3 gallons of milk and 5 shirts. The base year is 2019.

Year	Price of milk (per gallon)	Price of one shirt
2019	$3.25	$16.00
2020	$3.50	$16.50

(1) Compute the cost of the baskets in each year.

(2) Using the base year, compute the CPI in each year, rounding to the second decimal.

(3) Using the CPI from (2), compute the inflation rate for 2020.

---

[21] For more detail, see here: https://www.bls.gov/cpi/questions-and-answers.htm.

3. problems with the CPI

    a. _____ bias

        i. prices change at different _____. Consumers substitute

        into the relatively less expensive good

        ii. the CPI misses the substitution because of the _____

        nature of the basket

        iii.. therefore, the CPI will _____ the true change in

        the price level

    b. introduction of _____ goods

        i. the introduction of new goods increases _____,

        making each dollar more valuable

        ii. the CPI misses the new goods because of the _____ nature

        of the basket

        iii. therefore, the CPI will _____ the true change in the

        price level

    c. unmeasured _____ change

        i. _____ in quality increases the value of each dollar

        spent

        ii. these quality changes are difficult to measure so if

        improvements in quality are _____, the CPI will

        _____ the true change in the price level.

4. Core CPI

    a. definition: the CPI after removing _____ and _____ prices

b. food and energy prices are highly _____ so the price level

may be _____ skewed

    i. e.g. energy shocks

    ii. e.g. natural events such as floods

C. GDP Deflator

    1. definition: measures the prices of all goods and services produced

    _____

    2. GDP deflator $= (\frac{nominal\ GDP}{real\ GDP}) \times 100$

Class Exercise: **GDP Deflator**

Assume the base year is 2018.

Year	Nominal GDP	Real GDP
2018	$200	$200
2019	$600	$350
2020	$1,200	$500

(1) Find the GDP deflator for each year. Round to the second decimal.

(2) Find the inflation rate for 2019 and 2020. Round to the second decimal.

3. contrasting the CPI and GDP Deflator

    a. imported consumer goods

        i. _____ in CPI (if in basket)

        ii. _____ from GDP deflator

    b. capital goods

        i. _____ from CPI

        ii. _____ in GDP deflator (if produced domestically)

    c. the basket

        i. CPI uses a _____ basket

        ii. GDP deflator does _____ use a fixed basket

D. Personal Consumption Expenditures Price Index (PCEPI)

    1. definition: measures the change in prices paid for goods and services by

    _____ throughout the economy

        a. captures the _____ percentage change in prices across all

        categories within personal consumption expenditures[22]

        b. the FED _____ a 2 percent annual inflation rate as measured by

        PCEPI[23]

        c. there is also a _____ PCEPI measure

    2. contrasting the CPI and PCEPI

        a. measurement audience

            i. CPI: constructs a _____ consumer

---

[22] Personal consumption expenditures "measures the goods and services purchased by households and nonprofit institutions serving households. See https://www.bea.gov/national/pdf/NIPAhandbookch5.pdf for more information.
[23] See footnote 1 here http://www.federalreserve.gov/boarddocs/hh/2000/February/FullReport.pdf for reasoning why the FED focuses on PCE rather than CPI.

ii. PCEPI: _____ consumer purchases

b. the basket

i. CPI uses a _____ basket

ii. PCEPI _____ every quarter

iii. However, over ____ percent of the price data in PCEPI

overlaps with CPI

c. use

i. CPI: can use for cost-of-living-adjustments (COLA)

ii. PCEPI: not recommended for COLA since it changes every

quarter

E. Producer Price Index (PPI)

1. definition: measures the average change over time in the selling prices received

by domestic _____ for their output

2. measures sales at _____ levels of output, including non-finished goods

along the supply chain

a. often, changes in the PPI _____ changes in the CPI

F. Aggregate Price Level Summary

1. _____ these measurements are aggregate price levels

a. you can find inflation and deflation from each of them

2. _____ of these measurements are superior

a. it depends on what _____ you are asking

III. Comparing Dollar Figures Through Time

A. Introduction

1. a changing price level makes it _____ to compare dollar amounts from

different times

2. example: comparing the federal minimum wage through time

    a. $0.25 in 1938 and $7.25 in 2019

    b. did the federal minimum wage have more purchasing power in 1938

    or 2019?

        i. definition: purchasing power measures the _____ of goods

        and services a unit of currency can purchase

Amount in year you are changing into		Amount in year you are starting from	X	Price level from year changing into
	=			Price level from year starting from

        ii. in this example, the starting year is 1938 and the year we are

        changing the value into is 2019

        iii. the minimum wage = $0.25 in 1938 and $7.25 in 2019

        iv. the CPI in 1939 was 14.1 and the CPI in 2018 was 258.4

        v. ____ $= \$0.25 \times \dfrac{258.4}{14.1}$

            1. the minimum wage had a _____ purchasing

            power in 2019.

B. Indexation

    1. definition: a dollar amount is indexed for inflation if it is

        _____ corrected for inflation by law or in a contract

    2. examples include

        a. federal income tax brackets, Social Security payments, the minimum

        wage in some states

C. Is the cost of living and the standard of living the same concept?

1. _____!

   a. the _____ of living measures changes in _____.

   b. the _____ of living measures changes in _____ power.

Class Exercise: **Comparing Dollar Figures Through Time**

The table shows college tuition and required fees at all four-year institutions.

Year	Tuition	CPI
2014	$14,957	237.852
2018	$16,318	252.146
CPI numbers are from August of the listed year. Source: US Department of Education, National Center for Education Statistics. Table 330.10 found here:https://nces.ed.gov/programs/digest/d19/tables/dt19_330.10.asp?current=yes		

(1) Convert the 2014 tuition into 2018 dollars. Round to the nearest cent.

(2) Convert the 2018 tuition into 2014 dollars. Round to the nearest cent.

(3) Did students pay more for college in 2014 or 2018?

Topic Six: Saving and Investment

I. Introduction

    A. This lecture covers two broad issues

        1. The different types of _____

        2. How savings becomes investment through the _____ system

II. The Different Types of Saving

    A. Private Saving

        1. definition

            a. income minus _____ and _____

        2. calculation in the aggregate

            a. $Y - C - T$

        3. private savings can be _____ or _____

            a. if negative, the country is drawing down its _____ or

            _____ from abroad

    B. Public Saving

        1. definition

            a. tax _____ minus government _____

                i. for simplicity, taxes are net of transfers

        2. calculation in the aggregate

            a. $T - G$

        3. public savings can be positive or negative

            a. if _____, the country has a budget _____ and $T > G$

            b. if _____, the country has a budget _____ and $T < G$

C. National Saving

    1. definition

        a. _____ saving plus _____ saving

    2. calculation in the aggregate

        a. $(Y - C - T) + (T - G) => Y - C - G$

            i. national income that is not used for consumption or government purchases

III. Savings, Investment, and the Financial System

    A. Saving and Investment

        1. Start with national income accounting identity

            a. $Y = C + I + G + NX$

        2. For simplicity, assume a _____ economy

            a. $Y = C + I + G$

        3. Solve for I

            a. $I = Y - C - G$

                i. this is the same as national savings

            b. Saving = investment in a closed economy[24]

        4. savings is needed to purchase _____ capital and to _____ depreciated capital

        5. savings is _____ the same as investment

            a. savings is _____ consumption

            b. investment is the purchase of _____

        6. What does savings = investment mean?

---

[24] For the world, saving must equal investment.

a. in a closed economy, savings is an upper _____ for investment

i. a country may save more than it invests but it _____ invest more than it saves

6. for an economy open to the world, if investment is _____ than savings in a domestic market, the country is using foreign savings

a. e.g. foreign direct investment[25]

B. How Does Savings Become Investment

1. through the financial system

a. definition of financial system

i. the group of institutions _____ savings with investment

b. two broad sets of institutions

i. direct financing

1. definition: institutions where savers _____ provide funds to borrowers

a. e.g. buying _____ issued stock

ii. indirect financing

1. definition: institutions where savers _____ provide funds to borrowers

a. e.g.

2. examples of what households do with savings

---

[25] Foreign direct investment is capital investment by a foreigner in an affiliate in the domestic country. An affiliate is a business in which the foreign investor has a substantial interest, defined as ownership of at least ten percent of the voting stock of the business. See http://www.esa.doc.gov/sites/default/files/fdiesaissuebriefno2061411final_0.pdf for more detail.

a. purchase

    i. e.g.

b. deposit money

    i. e.g.

3. examples of how firms invest

    a. purchase _____ capital

       i. e.g.

    b. re-stock _____

    c. _____ capital improvement

       i. e.g.

    d. _____ and _____

Class Exercise: **Savings and Investment**

Suppose a closed economy where GDP = $10 trillion, consumption = $6.5 trillion, government purchases = $2 trillion, and a budget deficit of $300 billion.

(1) Find public saving.

(2) Find taxes.

(3) Find private saving.

(4) Find national saving.

(5) Find the investment of this economy.

Topic Seven: The Loanable Funds Market and the Real Interest Rate

I. Interest Rates

    A. Definition

        1. an interest rate is the _____ of _____ or the _____ to _____ rental funds

    B. Further Explanation

        1. an interest rate is the _____ for consuming _____ for the borrower or the _____ to consume _____ for the saver

        2. the interest rate _____ purchasing power by balancing _____ preferences and _____

    C. Types of Interest Rates

        1. nominal interest rate (N)

            a. definition: the rate of growth in the _____ value of a deposit or debt

            b. does not account for changes in the _____ level

            c. often, this is the interest rate you see

                i. e.g. interest rate for a mortgage or a savings account

        2. real interest rate (R)

            a. definition: the rate of growth in the _____ power of a deposit or debt

            b. accounts for _____ in the price level

            c. can calculate *ex* _____ and *ex* _____

                i. *ex ante* real interest rate

1. definition: the _____ interest rate minus the

_____ change in the price level

    a. using the Fisher identity

        i. $R = N - \pi^e$, where R is the real interest rate,

        N is the nominal interest rate, and π^e is the

        expected change in the aggregate price level

ii. *ex post* real interest rate

    1. definition: the _____ interest rate minus the

    _____ change in the price level

        a. using the Fisher identity

            i. $R = N - \pi$, where R is the real interest rate,

            N is the nominal interest rate, and π is the

            actual change in the aggregate price level

II. The Market for Loanable Funds

    A. Introduction

        1. a supply and demand model that determines a representative _____ interest rate in the economy in the _____

            a. definition of long-run

                i. when prices _____ adjust to changes in supply and demand

            b. the real interest rate, _____ the nominal interest rate, matters for savings and investment decisions because the real rate determines purchasing power

2. loanable funds definition

    a. the flow of _____ available to fund _____

    investment

B. Model

    1. assumptions

        a. _____ financial market

        b. all _____ deposit their savings in this market

        c. all _____ borrow from this market

        d. _____ representative real interest rate

    2. The supply of loanable funds represents the supply of _____

        a. a _____ interest rate makes savings more

        _____, increasing the quantity supplied of loanable funds,

    ceteris paribus.

    3. factors shifting the supply curve

        a. changes in _____ savings

            i. changes in _____

                1. e.g. As income _____ (falls), savings

_____ (decrease).

    ii. changes in consumer _____

        1. e.g. As people become _____ (more) confident in

        the direction of the economy, they save _____ (less)

    iii. _____

        1. e.g. people become more (less) _____, saving

        more (less)

    iv. _____

        1. e.g. the economy has more _____

        adults, savings increases

        2. e.g. the economy has more _____ people, savings

        decreases

    v. _____

        1. e.g. tax credit to make savings more _____

        increases savings

        2. e.g. increasing taxes on savings, like earned _____

        or _____ gains, decreases savings

    vi. If private savings _____, the supply curve shifts down

    and to the _____. If private savings _____, the

    supply curve shifts up and to the _____.

b. changes in _____ savings

    i. e.g. if the government runs a budget _____, public

    savings _____

ii. e.g. if the government runs a budget _____, public

savings _____

iii. Like private savings, if public savings _____, the

supply curve shifts down and to the _____. If public savings

_____, the supply curve shifts up and to the _____.

4. the demand for loanable funds represents the demand for _____

    a. there are _____ sources of demand

        i. _____ borrowing

        ii. _____ borrowing

        iii. _____ borrowing

    b. a _____ interest rate reduces the cost of _____,

increasing the quantity demanded of loanable funds, *ceteris paribus.*

5. factors shifting the demand curve

    a. expectations of future _____

        i. e.g. if firms expect _____ (lower) profits, they will

invest _____ (less)

    b. new _____

i. e.g. new technology _____ the _____ of

production, _____ the demand for investment

c. _____

    i. e.g. a tax _____ to spur investment, _____ the

    demand for investment

    ii. e.g. a tax increase on _____ decreases the demand for

    investment

d. government _____

    i. e.g. more government borrowing _____ demand for

    loanable funds

e. If demand for loanable funds _____, the demand curve shifts

up and to the _____. If demand for loanable funds _____,

the demand curve shifts down and to the _____.

6. Equilibrium

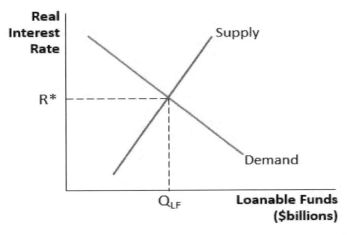

a. the interest rate _____ to equate supply and demand

    i. in equilibrium, $Q_D = Q_S$ of loanable funds

b. if the interest rate is _____ the equilibrium, $Q_D > Q_S$

    i. the interest rate _____

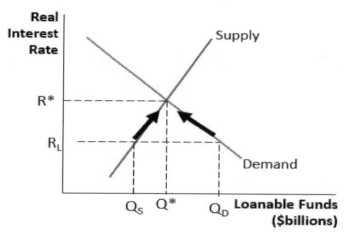

c. if the interest rate is _____ the equilibrium, $Q_S > Q_D$

    i. the interest rate _____

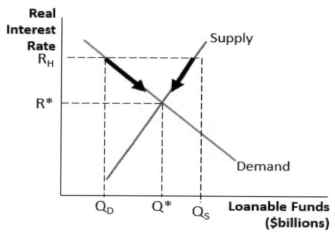

7. Model in Action

    a. increase in savings

        i. Anything that increases savings increases the supply of loanable funds

        ii. the interest rate _____ and the quantity of loanable funds

        _____

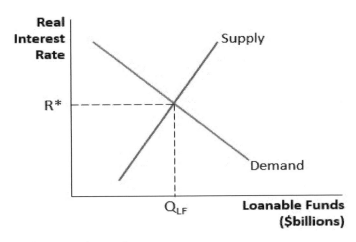

b. decrease in savings

    i. Anything that decreases savings decreases the supply of loanable

funds

    ii. the interest rate _____ and the quantity of loanable funds

_____

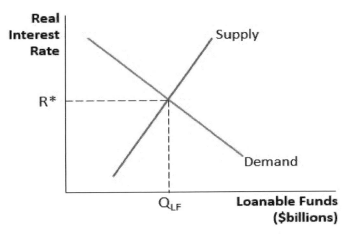

c. a special case: budget deficits and crowding-out

    i. a budget deficit _____ national saving, shifting the supply

curve left

    ii. the interest rate _____ and the amount of loanable

funds available for _____ investment _____

    iii. the decrease in _____ spending (in this case private

investment) when government spending increases is called

_____

      iv. _____ deficits lead to a rising government debt

d. an increase in borrowing

      i. anything that increases the desire to borrow increases the demand of loanable funds

      ii. the interest rate _____ and the quantity of loanable funds

_____

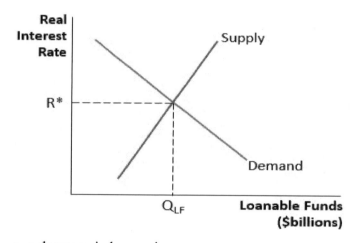

e. a decrease in borrowing

      i. anything that decreases the desire to borrow decreases the demand for loanable funds

      ii. the interest rate _____ and the quantity of loanable funds

_____

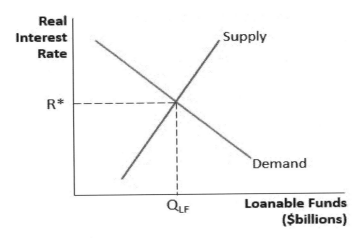

8. Never reason from a price change

   a. True, false, or uncertain. If the real interest rate falls, will investment

   increase? Explain.

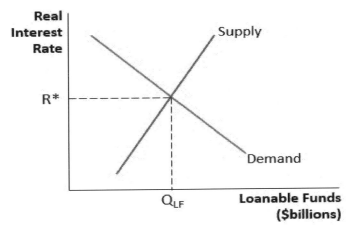

   i. if savings increases, the supply of loanable funds shifts right, the

   interest rate falls, and investment increases

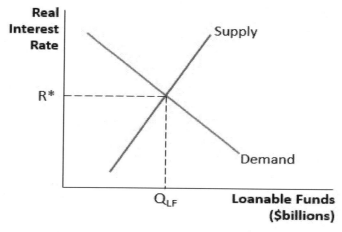

ii. if demand decreases, the demand of loanable funds shifts left,

the interest rate falls, and investment decreases

b. lesson

i. start with what _____ the interest rate to change,

_____ reason what happens to investment and the interest rate.

Topic Eight: The Liquidity Preference Model and the Nominal Interest Rate

I. Introduction

A. The Importance of Money

1. without money trade requires _____

a. definition of barter

i. the _____ of one good or service for another

2. every transaction requires a _____ _____ of wants

a. definition of double coincidence of wants

i. when two people _____ have a good or service the _____ wants

3. money makes trade more _____ by lowering the _____ of transactions

B. What is Money

    1. definition

        a. _____ that is _____ accepted in

        _____ for goods and services or in the _____ of

        debts

    2. important: money is _____ the same as wealth or income[26]

    3. typically, when the economy is _____, people accept _____

    things as money. When the economy is _____, people prefer more

    _____ forms of money, like currency

C. Three Functions of Money

    1. medium of exchange

        a. _____ acceptable means of _____

            i. this is the most _____ function of money

    2. unit of account

        a. how people post _____ and record _____

    3. store of value

        a. a transfer of _____ power through time

D. Two Kinds of Money

    1. commodity money

        a. definition: money with _____ value

            i. definition of intrinsic value

                1. the commodity has value as something _____ than

---

[26] Wealth is the total collection of assets that serve to store value. Income is the flow of earnings over time. Liquidity is the relative ease and speed with which an asset can be converted into a medium of exchange.

money

  ii. e.g.

2. fiat money

  a. definition: money _____ intrinsic value

   i. e.g.

E. Money Supply

 1. definition

  a. the group of _____ assets that households and businesses can use

 to make _____ or to hold as short term _____

 2. There are _____ measurements of the money supply. The money

supply is not just currency.

 3. U.S. money supply measurements from narrowest to broadest

  a. currency

   i. definition: paper _____ and _____

  b. monetary base

   i. definition: sum of _____ and bank _____

  held at the central bank

  c. M1

   i. definition: sum of _____, _____

  deposits, and _____ checks

  d. M2

   i. definition: sum of M1 plus _____ deposits, small

  time deposits, and retail money market mutual funds

F. Money Demand

    1. definition

        a. _____ holding of financial assets in the form of _____

    2. people hold money for _____ reasons

        a.

        b.

        c.

    3. money demand is a _____ made by individuals

II. Theory of Liquidity Preferences

    A. Introduction

        1. a supply and demand model that determines a representative _____

        interest rate in the economy in the _____

            a. for simplicity, assume peopled store wealth in either _____

            or _____

        2. the simplest model assumes the central bank _____ controls the money

        supply at a _____ amount

            a. the money supply shifts _____ (left) when the central bank

            _____ (decreases) the money supply

            b. the money supply can also increase (decrease) as the number of money

            _____ increases (decreases)

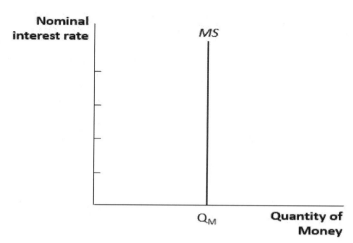

3. money demand

   a. At higher interest rates, the _____ cost of holding

money increases. People hold _____ money so the money

demand curve _____ downwards.

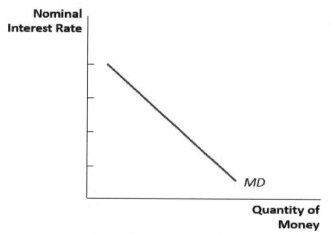

   b. money demand shifts for _____ reasons

      i. change in _____

         1. as income _____, people want to hold more money

as a store of _____ and to increase _____

      ii. change in the _____

         1. as the price-level _____, people need to hold

more money to keep _____ constant

iii. _____

          1. some people prefer to hold more (less) money

B. Model in Action

    1. the interest rate _____ to equate money supply and money demand

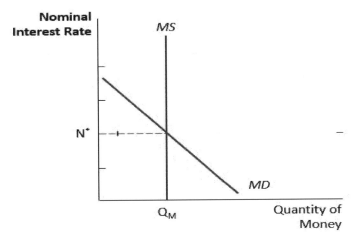

    2. example: suppose income increases

        a. the interest rate _____ and the quantity of money stays the _____

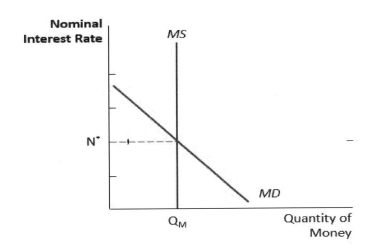

    3. example: the central bank increases the money supply

        a. the interest rate _____ and the quantity of money _____

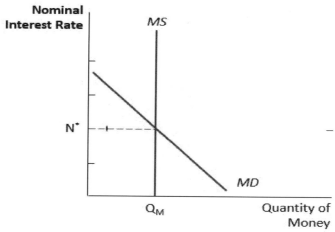

C. Expansionary Monetary Policy and Interest Rates

    1. does increasing the money supply increase or decrease nominal interest rates?

        a. _____, depending on the time frame

    2. four factors

        a. _____ effect

        b. _____ effect

        c. _____ _____ effect

        d. _____ _____ effect

    3. liquidity effect

        a. nominal interest rates should _____ if the money supply increases

            i. an increase in the money supply makes _____ money

            available in the economy

        b. this is a _____ effect

    4. Income effect

        a. Nominal interest rates should _____ if the money supply increases.

        This is a _____ effect.

            i. an increase in the money supply _____ the economy via

the liquidity effect

    1. this has _____ effects

        a. money _____ increases as consumers make more

        _____

        b. firms _____ more, increasing the supply of bonds, lowering bond prices and increasing the interest rates of bonds[27]

5. Price-level effect

    a. Nominal interest rates should _____ if the money supply increases. This is a _____ effect.

        i. an increase in the money supply _____ prices in the long-run (i.e. the Quantity Theory of Money)

        ii. when prices increase, people increase their money _____ to keep consumption _____

6. Expected-inflation effect

    a. Nominal interest rates should _____ if the money supply increases. This is a _____ effect.

        i. an increase in inflation increases inflation _____

        ii. people will _____ higher interest rates via the Fisher identity

---

[27] See appendix 1 for an explanation of the inverse relationship between bond prices and the interest rate on bonds.

Topic Nine: The Banking System and Money Creation

I. Introduction

    A. The Banking System

        1. the modern banking system is a _____ reserve banking system

            a. definition of fractional reserve banking system

                i. a banking system where banks keep a fraction of _____

                as _____ and can _____ the rest

            b. definition of deposits

                i. deposits are a sum of money _____ in a bank account

            c. definition of reserves

                i. reserves are bank deposits that are _____ lent[28]

        2. banks help determine the size of the _____ money supply

    measurements by creating _____ money

II. Bank's Role in Money Creation

    A. How Banks Create Deposit Money

        1. The Bank T-Account

            a. definition: an accounting statement showing a bank's _____ and

            _____

        2. reserve ratio (R)

            a. definition: the _____ of deposits kept in reserves by a bank

            rather than being lent

            b. prior to March 26, 2020, the Federal Reserve required banks to hold

---

[28] See here for the statement on the policy eliminating these requirements:
https://www.federalreserve.gov/monetarypolicy/reservereq.htm.

reserve requirements

c. banks can now _____ how much to keep in reserves

    i. banks keep reserves to conduct daily business and to prevent

    _____

3. example of a T-Account

First National Bank			
Assets		Liabilities	
Reserves	$10	Deposits	$100
Loans	$90		

    i. in this example, notice that R = ($10 / $100) x 100 =

    _____%

4. Fractional Reserve Banks and the Broader Money Supply: An Example

    a. Suppose First National Bank (FNB) loans all but 10% of its deposits in reserves.

        i. initial T-account of FNB

First National Bank			
Assets		Liabilities	
Reserves	$100	Deposits	$100
Loans	$0		

        ii. final T-account of FNB

First National Bank			
Assets		Liabilities	
Reserves	$10	Deposits	$100
Loans	$90		

        iii. money supply = _____, $100 in deposits and $90 in currency

b. Suppose the borrower deposits the $90 at Second National Bank (SNB)

    i. initial T-account of SNB

Second National Bank			
Assets		Liabilities	
Reserves	$90	Deposits	$90
Loans	$0		

    ii. if R = 10% for SNB, it will loan all but 10% of the deposit

    iii. final T-account of SNB

Second National Bank			
Assets		Liabilities	
Reserves	$9	Deposits	$90
Loans	$81		

c. Suppose the borrower deposits the $81 at Third National Bank

(TNB)

    i. initial T-account of TNB

Third National Bank			
Assets		Liabilities	
Reserves	$81	Deposits	$81
Loans	$0		

    ii. if R = 10% for TNB, it will loan all but 10% of the deposit

    iii. final T-account of TNB

Third National Bank			
Assets		Liabilities	
Reserves	$8.10	Deposits	$81
Loans	$72.90		

d. the process continues, and money is created with each new loan

Original deposit	$100
FNB lending	$90
SNB lending	$81
TNB lending	$72.90
...	...
Total money supply	$1,000.00

       i. in this example, $100 of _____ generates $1000 of

      _____

3. The Money Multiplier

    a. definition

       i. the amount of money the banking system can _____

      with each dollar of reserves

    b. the money multiplier equals _____

       i. in our example, R = 10%

$$\text{1. money multiplier} = \frac{1}{R} => \frac{1}{0.1} = 10$$

      2. $100 of reserves can create 10 x $100 = _____ of money

Class Exercise: **Money Multiplier and the Reserve Ratio**

(1) Suppose a bank keeps 10 percent of its deposits in reserves and the bank has $5000 in deposits. How much are reserves and how much did the bank lend?

(2) Suppose a bank has $10,000 in deposits and $8,000 in loans. How large is the bank's reserve ratio?

(3) Using Table 1, answer the following. What is the bank's reserve ratio? What is the money multiplier? What is the maximum amount of money the bank can create with $10,000 of new reserves?

Table 1

TKC Bank

	Assets		Liabilities
Reserves	$10,000	Deposits	$25,000
Loans	$15,000		

Topic Ten: The Federal Reserve and Monetary Policy

I. The Structure and Goals of the Federal Reserve

    A. Introduction

        1. definition of central bank

            a. an institution that oversees the _____ system and

            conducts _____ policy

        2. the _____ _____ (FED) is the central bank of the U.S.

        3. definition of monetary policy

            a. the _____ of central banks to achieve their macroeconomic policy

            _____

        4. monetary policy can be _____ or _____

            a. expansionary monetary policy definition

                i. when the central bank _____ the economy by

_____ interest rates and/or _____ the

money supply

b. expansionary monetary policy is designed to _____ economic

growth, employment, and inflation

c. contractionary monetary policy definition

i. when the central bank slows the economy by _____

interest rates and/or _____ the money supply

d. contractionary monetary policy is designed to _____ economic

growth and _____ the inflation rate

5. Dual Mandate of the FED[29]

a. stable aggregate _____

i. an inflation rate of _____, as measured by the personal

consumption expenditures price index, year over year change[30,31]

1. the 2% goals is _____

b. maximum level of _____

i. the FED estimates a _____ for the long-run normal level of

the unemployment rate, the unemployment rate that keeps inflation

_____ (i.e. the lowest unemployment rate the

---

[29] See here for more detail: https://www.federalreserve.gov/faqs/money_12848.htm.

[30] Measured by the year-over-year percent change in the Personal Consumption Expenditures: Chain-Price Type Index (PCEPI). The FED focuses on this aggregate price level because "the PCE index covers a wide range of household spending." See here: https://www.federalreserve.gov/faqs/economy_14419.htm.

[31] The FED uses a two percent inflation target because "…a higher inflation rate would reduce the public's ability to make accurate longer-term economic and financial decision…[while] a lower inflation rate would be associated with an elevated probability of falling into deflation, which means prices and perhaps wages, on average, are falling, a phenomenon associated with very weak economic conditions." See here: https://www.federalreserve.gov/faqs/economy_14400.htm.

economy can sustain without accelerating inflation)[32]

    c. these two goals will keep _____ interest rates at a moderate level

    d. the FED's goals of maximum employment and 2 percent inflation are generally _____

        i. if inflation is below the 2% objective and the unemployment rate is above the long-run normal level, the FED will pursue _____ monetary policy

        ii. if inflation is above the 2% objective and the unemployment rate is below the long-run normal level, the FED will pursue _____ monetary policy

    e. what happens if the goals are _____ complementary?

        i. e.g. inflation is below 2 percent and the unemployment rate is below the long-run normal level

        ii. e.g. inflation is above 2 percent and the unemployment rate is above the long-run normal level

        iii. the FED pursues a _____ approach that focuses on the part of the mandate that is further from its objective

B. The Structure of the FED[33]

    1. the Federal Reserve System consists of

---

[32] The FED does not target a specific rate of employment. See here: https://www.federalreserve.gov/faqs/what-economic-goals-does-federal-reserve-seek-to-achieve-through-monetary-policy.htm. Additionally, since the normal rate of unemployment is an estimate that changes as structural factors in the economy change, the employment target is not fixed like the 2 percent inflation target. Here is the explanation from the FED: "The maximum level of employment is largely determined by nonmonetary factors that affect the structure and dynamics of the job market. These factors may change over time and may not be directly measurable. As a result, the FOMC does not specify a fixed goal for maximum employment; rather, the FOMC's policy decisions must be informed by its members' assessments of the maximum level of employment, though such assessments are necessarily uncertain and subject to revision."

[33] See here for more detail: https://www.federalreserve.gov/aboutthefed/structure-federal-reserve-system.htm.

a. _____ regional FED banks

b. Board of Governors (BOG)

    i. _____ members

    ii. each member is nominated by the _____ and

    confirmed by the _____

    iii. a full term is _____ years

    iv. the BOG changes the _____ rate and _____

    rates on reserves

c. Federal Open Market Committee (FOMC)

    i. includes the members of the _____ and _____ presidents from

    the regional FED banks.

        1. the presidents of the regional FED banks rotate on and

        off the FOMC, except for the president of the New York

        FED bank, who is always on the FOMC

    ii. conducts _____ market operations.

    iii. meets _____ times per year

    iv. _____ _____ is the current chair of the FOMC

D. Independence of the FED

    1. the FED is under the _____ of Congress and the President

    2. however, for purposes of _____ , the FED operates

    _____

        a. Congress and the President do not directly _____ with

    monetary policy decision

b. interference by politicians _____ the credibility of central banks

because _____ observers may interpret the bank's actions as

_____, not economic

   3. there are two strong arguments _____ an independent FED

      a. the FED should be held _____ accountable by voters

      b. the FED has pursued _____ monetary policy at times

II. Tools of the Federal Reserve[34]

   A. Tools of Monetary Policy

      1. open-market operations

         a. definition: the purchase and sale, temporary or permanent, of U.S.

         _____ bonds and notes

         b. this _____ the FED's tool of _____ when the FED mainly

         changed the money base to conduct monetary policy

         c. to _____ the monetary base, and by extension the broader

         money supply, the FED _____ government bonds, paying with

         _____ money

         d. to _____ the monetary base, and by extension the broader

         money supply, the FED _____ government bonds, taking money

         _____ of circulation

         e. examples with T-Accounts

            i. suppose the FED wants to _____ the monetary base and

            purchases $10 billion of Treasury bonds from banks

               1. the banking system T-Account changes

---

[34] See here for more detail: https://www.federalreserve.gov/aboutthefed/files/pf_3.pdf

Banking System T-Account			
Assets		Liabilities	
Treasury Bonds	- $10 billion		
Reserves	+ $10 billion		

2. the FED T-Account changes

Federal Reserve T-Account			
Assets		Liabilities	
Treasury Bonds	+ $10 billion	Reserves	+ $10 billion

ii. suppose the FED wants to _____ the monetary base and

sells $10 billion of Treasury bonds to banks

1. the banking system T-Account changes

Banking System T-Account			
Assets		Liabilities	
Treasury Bonds	+ $10 billion		
Reserves	- $10 billion		

2. the FED T-Account changes

Federal Reserve T-Account			
Assets		Liabilities	
Treasury Bonds	- $10 billion	Reserves	- $10 billion

e. the FED uses this tool to target the _____ _____ rate by

changing the _____ of balances in the federal funds market

i. banks can borrow overnight _____ from other banks

ii. definition of federal funds rate

1. the federal funds rate is the interest rate on _____

loans of _____ between banks

iii. starting in 2008, the FED targets a _____ rather than a specific rate

iv. interest rates are highly _____, so changes in the

federal funds rate influences other short-term interest rates

2. the discount rate

a. definition

i. the interest rate on loans the _____ makes to _____

b. the FED is the lender of _____ resort

i. when banks are running low on reserves, they may _____

reserves from the FED

c. to encourage banks to borrow more reserves from the Fed, the FED

_____ the discount rate

d. to discourage banks from borrowing more reserves from the Fed, the

FED _____ the discount rate

3. Large-scale Asset Purchases

a. definition

i. the purchase of _____ securities issued by the U.S.

government and longer-termed securities issued or guaranteed by

government-sponsored agencies

b. e.g. long-term Treasury bonds and mortgage backed securities

c. informally known as _____ _____ (QE)

d. is an _____ of open-market operations that the FED uses when

the federal funds rate approaches _____

e. QE raises asset prices, which makes people feel _____,

which increases spending and stimulates the economy

4. forward guidance

    a. definition

        i. the FED provides _____ about its _____

        for the _____ of the federal funds rate

    b. used to influence _____ about the _____

    course of monetary policy

    c. if the FED signals a _____ federal funds rate, it is signaling

    _____ monetary policy

    d. if the FED signals a _____ federal funds rate, it is signaling

    _____ monetary policy

5. paying interest on reserves

    a. definition

        i. the FED pays banks interest on bank reserves

    b. this policy started in October 2008

    c. Paying interest on reserves is the FED's _____ monetary policy of

    choice. It affects how much reserves banks are willing to hold by changing

    the _____ for reserves.

    d. banks have no incentive to lend reserves at an interest rate _____

    the interest rate on reserves, giving the FED more _____ over the

    federal funds rate

    e. the interest on reserves acts like a _____ for the top end of the

    federal funds range

f. however, _____ all financial firms can keep reserves at the FED

6. reverse repurchases[35]

    a. definition

        i. the FED _____ a security to a financial institution and

        promises to purchase it at a specific price the _____ day

    b. the price the FED pays is an _____ rate

    c. the FED sets this rate at the _____ of its federal funds rate range

    to give the FED more control of the federal funds rate

        i. financial institutions have no incentive to lend at an interest rate

        _____ this rate so this interest rate acts like a _____

    for the bottom end of the federal funds range

III. A Graphical View of Monetary Policy

    A. The Market for Reserves Model

    1. a supply and demand model of _____ that determines the _____

    _____rate

    a. on the _____ axis is the federal funds rate

    b. on the _____ axis is the quantity of reserves

    2. the demand curve

    a. As the federal funds rate _____, the _____

    _____ of holding reserves falls. Therefore, the demand curve for

    reserves slopes _____.

    b. Once the federal funds rate _____ the interest rate the FED pays

    for reverse repurchases, financial institutions would _____ lend reserves

---

[35] For more detail, see here: https://www.newyorkfed.org/aboutthefed/fedpoint/fed04.html.

in the federal funds market and would _____ reserves indefinitely, making

the demand curve perfectly _____ at this point.

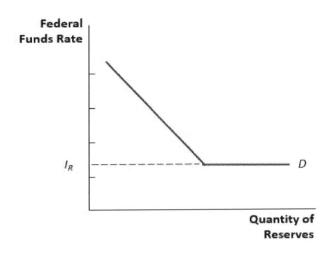

3. the supply curve

    a. the supply of reserves includes _____ reserves and

    _____ reserves

        i. nonborrowed reserves definition

            1. reserves the _____ supplies via open-market operations

        ii. borrowed reserves definition

            1. reserves _____ borrow from the FED (e.g. through

            the discount window)

    b. since the FED determines the nonborrowed reserves, this part of the

    supply curve is perfectly _____

    c. The FED sets the discount rate _____ than the federal funds rate.

    If the federal funds rate is lower than the discount rate, banks will not

    borrow reserves from the FED.

    d. If the federal funds rate is _____ than the discount rate, banks

    would borrow an _____ amount of reserves from the FED to

lend to other banks in the federal funds market. Therefore, the supply

curve is perfectly _____ at the discount rate.

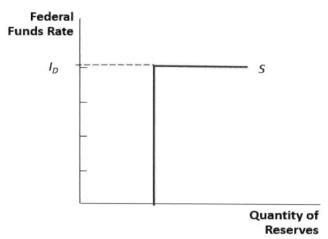

4. equilibrium

   a. in equilibrium, the supply of reserves _____ the demand for reserves

   b. The FED will keep the interest paid on reverse repurchases _____

   than the federal funds rate to act like a _____. Therefore, unless the

   interest rates on reverse repurchases and the federal funds rate are the

   _____, the supply curve intersects the demand curve on

   the _____ sloping part of the demand curve.

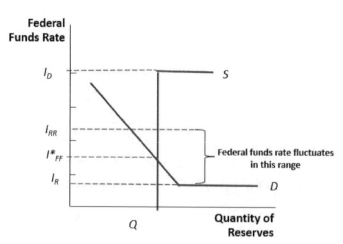

B. The Model in Action

1. open-market operations

    a. if the FED _____ bonds, the _____ of reserves increases,

    _____ the federal funds rate and _____ the quantity

of reserves

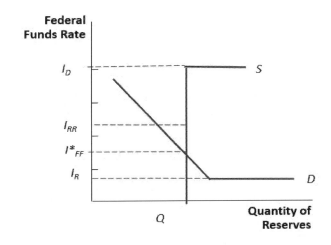

    b. if the FED _____ bonds, the _____ of reserves decreases,

    _____ the federal funds rate and _____ the quantity

of reserves

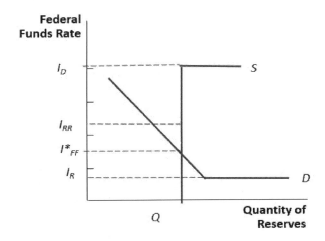

2. large-scale asset purchases

    a. if the federal funds and the interest rate of reverse repurchases are the

_____, increasing the supply of reserves will _____ change the federal

funds rate but will increase the quantity of reserves

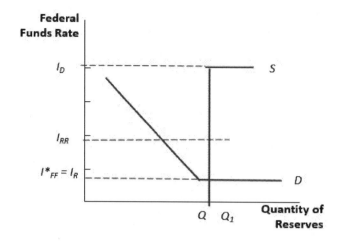

b. This situation is when large-scale asset purchases make _____. The

FED _____ stimulate the economy through measures _____ than

changing the federal funds rate.

3. discount rate

a. since the FED keeps the discount rate above the federal funds rate as a

matter of policy, a decrease in the discount rate will _____ change the

federal funds rate or the quantity of reserves

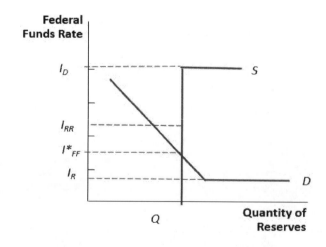

b. an increase in the discount rate will also _____ change the federal funds

rate or the quantity of reserves

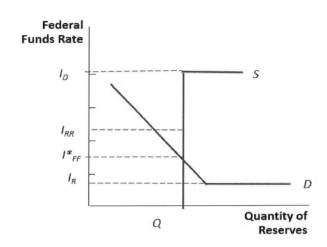

4. reverse repurchases

    a. if the interest rate on reverse repurchases and the federal funds rate are

the _____ , increasing the interests on reverse repurchases

_____ the federal funds rate

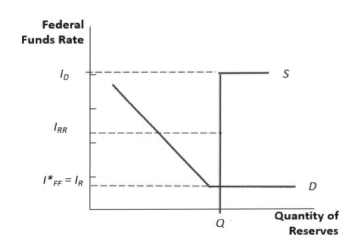

IV. Difficulties of Monetary Policy

    A. Three Difficulties

        1. The FED operates in _____ _____ with _____ knowledge

        2. The FED's control of monetary aggregates _____ than the monetary base is

        _____ and subject to _____

a. the FED uses _____ _____ to reduce lags and

help individuals and businesses make more informed spending and

investment decisions[36]

3. Negative _____ _____ dilemma (future lecture)

a. the FED does _____ control productivity

B. Takeaway

1. these three problems can cause the FED to _____ or

_____ their intended monetary policy objective[37]

V. Monetary Policy Regimes

A. Two Regimes

1. discretionary policy

a. definition: the central bank makes no _____ to future

actions but acts in the moment according to changing economic conditions

2. rules-based policy

a. definition: the central bank follows a consistent policy known in

_____

B. Which Regime?

1. the case for discretion

a. _____

2. the case for rules

a. builds _____

b. central banks are held _____

---

[36] For more detail on forward guidance, see here: https://www.federalreserve.gov/faqs/what-is-forward-guidance-how-is-it-used-in-the-federal-reserve-monetary-policy.htm.

[37] Overshooting is providing too much stimulus. Undershooting is providing too little stimulus.

Topic Eleven: Money Growth and Inflation

I. Monetary Equilibrium

    A. Money Supply and Demand Model

        1. introduction

            a. a model graphically showing how changes in money supply and money demand change the aggregate _____ level

            b. the _____ axis is the _____ of money

                i. in the simple model, only changes in the money _____ change the quantity of money

            c. there are _____ vertical axes: value of money and price level

                i. the value of money is the _____ of the price level

        2. graphical representation

            a. a _____ in the value of money _____ the quantity of money demanded

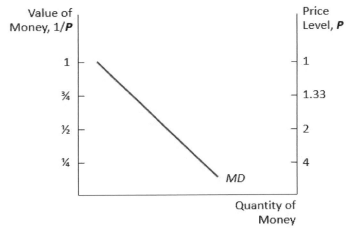

            b. for simplicity, assume the money supply is _____ by the central bank (i.e. vertical)

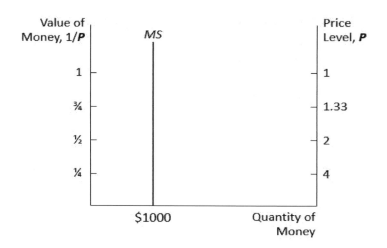

c. The price level (P) adjusts to equate money supply and money demand

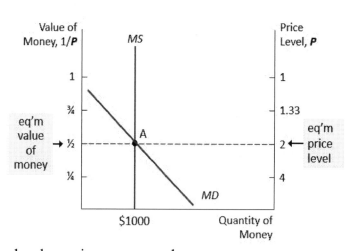

3. example: change in money supply

a. suppose the FED increases the money supply

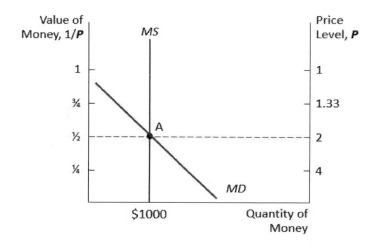

a. the value of money _____, the price level _____, and the

quantity of money increases

3. example: change in money demand

a. suppose money demand increases

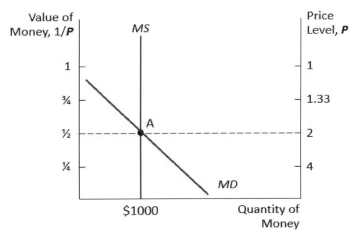

a. the value of money _____, the price level _____, and the

quantity of money does not change

II. The Quantity Theory of Money

A. Introduction

1. definition

a. a _____ model that explains the _____ cause of how

the aggregate price level changes

2. "Inflation is always and everywhere a monetary phenomenon." ~ Milton

Friedman, 1976 Nobel Prize winner in economics

B. Terminology

1. M is money _____

a. e.g. the monetary _____

2. MD is money _____

3. Y is _____ output

    a. i.e. real _____

4. P is the _____ price level

5. k is the _____ of _____ people want to hold as money

    a. i.e. a measurement of money _____

6. V is _____

    a. definition: the _____ of times a unit of money is _____ per year

    b. velocity is the _____ of the percentage of income people hold as money

        i. i.e. the inverse of money demand

    b. An _____ (decrease) in _____ means _____ increases (decreases). We spend money (M) on output (Y) and since Y = C + I + G + NX, if velocity (V) changes, then C, I, G, or N must change.

    c. _____ and _____ features change velocity. If people can make more transactions without money (e.g. credit cards), less money is demanded, and vice versa. These institutional and technological features tend to change _____ through time so velocity is relatively stable.

C. Model in Action

    1. in equilibrium, _____ = _____

    2. MD = _____, where k = _____

3. By substitution

    a. M =

    b. M =

4. Rearrange

    a. M x V = P x Y

        i. called the _____ equation

        ii. MV = total _____

            1. how much money we have in total (M) times how many times we spent the money (V) represents the actions of

            _____

        iii. PY = _____ output

            1. the goods and services we produce and sell (Y) times the prices we charge (P) represents the actions of _____

5. The Quantity Theory in Steps

    a. rearrange the Exchange Equation as $P = \dfrac{M \, x \, V}{Y}$

    b. there are _____ causes that can change P

        i. changes in M, V, or Y

    c. Y and V do not change much each year, so they are _____ explanations for large and sustained changes in P over time

        i. e.g. real GDP rarely increases or decreases 10% a year

    d. the only variable left to change P is _____

        i. the primary cause of changes in the price level over time is changes in the money _____

e. can also write the Exchange Equation in _____ rates[38]:

$\vec{M} + \vec{V} = \vec{P} + \vec{Y}$, where the arrows over the variables designate the

growth rate of the variable

      i. if V and Y are _____ changing, the growth rate of M is

      _____ to the growth rate of prices

      ii. if M is growing _____ than money demand and output,

      prices _____

      iii. if M is growing _____ than money demand and output,

      prices _____

6. Does money change real output in the long-run?

    a. _____! Think back to the Solow Model. Only changes in real

variables, institutions, and technology change output over time.

      i. definition of real variables

         1. variables measured in physical units and when expressed

         in dollar terms, are adjusted for changes in the price level

      ii. examples of real variables include factors of production: land,

      labor, and capital

      iii. definition of nominal variables

         1. variables expressed in dollar terms _____ adjusted for

         changes in the price level

D. Summary

    1. central bank policy is the _____ driver of changes in the price level

---

[38] When written in levels, M x V = total expenditures and P x Y = total income. Using the property that if X = A x B, then the growth rate of X is approximately equal to the growth rate in A plus the growth rate in B.

since it is the principal cause of changes in the money supply

2. in the long-run, money is _____

    a. definition of money neutrality

        i. changes in the money supply _____ change aggregate prices

        and leave relative prices and output unchanged

    b. Why? Production only changes when _____ variables change

III. Money in the Economy

    A. The Adjustment Process

        1. how does increasing the money supply increase the price level?

        a. a monetary injection causes an _____ in the supply of

        money at the _____ price level

Value of Money, $1/P$ — MS — Price Level, P

1, ¾, ½ (A), ¼ — MD — 1, 1.33, 2, 4

$1000 — Quantity of Money

    b. the excess money is _____

        i. additional _____ and _____

    c. the monetary injection does _____ increase an economy's long-term

    _____ capacity

    d. There is more money chasing the same amount of goods and

    services so the price level _____.

Class Exercise: **Quantity Theory of Money**

(1) Consider the Exchange Equation in levels (i.e. M x V = P x Y). If the money supply is $100 billion, the price level is 5, and real GDP is $25 billion, what is velocity?

(2) Consider the Exchange Equation in levels (i.e. M x V = P x Y). If velocity is 5 and nominal GDP is $20 billion, how large is the money supply?

(3) Consider the Exchange Equation in growth rates (i.e. $\vec{M} + \vec{V} = \vec{P} + \vec{Y}$). If the money supply grows at 6% and velocity grows at 1 percent, how much does nominal GDP grow?

Topic Twelve: Inflation and Deflation

I. The Inflation Fallacy

    A. Definition

        1. the fallacy that inflation erodes _____ income at the _____

        level

    B. Why is this a fallacy

        1. inflation increases the prices of the things people buy _____ sell so one

        person's price increase is another person's income increase

            a. suffers from the fallacy of _____

        2. in the _____ run, money is _____ and income is determined by

        real factors like _____

II. Cost of Inflation

    A. Seven Costs of Inflation

1. the inflation tax

    a. definition: when inflation reduces the purchasing power of money

    _____

2. shoe leather costs

    a. definition: the resources wasted when people _____ their money

    holdings

3. menu costs

    a. definition: the direct and managerial costs of _____ prices

4. misallocation of resources

    a. firms do not raise prices _____ so _____

    prices change, _____ resource allocation, particularly the

    capital structure

5. confusion and inconvenience

    a. inflation makes it difficult to _____ dollar amounts over

    _____ so long-term planning is difficult

6. tax distortions

    a. some taxes are based on _____ income rather than _____

    income, _____ the tax bill

7. redistribution of wealth

    a. if inflation is _____ than expected _____ gain

    at the expense of creditors

    b. if inflation is _____ than expected _____ gain

    at the expense of borrowers

Class Exercise: **Tax Distortions and Inflation**

For questions (1) through (5) you deposit $1,000 in a bank for one year, the tax rate on nominal interest gained is 25%, the nominal interest rate is 10%, and there is no inflation.

(1) By how much did the nominal value of your deposit grow in dollar terms?

(2) By how much did the real value of your deposit grow in dollar terms?

(3) How much did you pay in taxes?

(4) What is the after-tax nominal interest rate?

(5) What is the after-tax real interest rate?

For questions (6) through (10) you deposit $1,000 in a bank for one year, the tax rate on nominal interest gained is 25%, the nominal interest rate is 20%, and the inflation rate is 10%.

(6) By how much did the nominal value of your deposit grow in dollar terms?

(7) By how much did the real value of your deposit grow in purchasing power terms?

(8) How much did you pay in taxes, if nominal income is taxed?

(9) What is the after-tax nominal interest rate?

(10) What is the after-tax real interest rate?

III. Hyperinflation

    A. Definition

        1. an increase in the aggregate price level of at least _____% per month

    B. Examples

        1.

    C. Dangers of Hyperinflation

        1. high inflation is more _____ and _____ predictable than low

        inflation

            a. exacerbates the seven costs of inflation (see above)

        2. high inflation erodes _____ in public institutions, making

        monetary policy more difficult and less effective

    D. Takeaway

        1. excessive growth in the money supply _____ causes hyperinflation

IV. Benefits of Low and Stable Inflation

    A. Two Benefits

        1. prevents dynamic _____ due to wage and price _____

            a. definition of dynamic inefficiency

                i. when markets do _____ clear over time because of some

                _____

            b. definition of sticky prices

                i. prices that do not change _____ to changes in supply and

                demand

            c. sticky prices _____ markets from clearing

d. labor market example

  i. suppose inflation is _____, the economy enters a recession, and nominal spending decreases

  ii. facing a lower demand, firms' _____ decline

  iii. firms must _____ costs to keep the same profit margin

  iv. firms lay off _____ or pay lower _____ since it is often easier to reduce labor than capital

  v. if _____ workers in the economy accepted pay cuts, firms' costs fall the same as revenue, keeping profit margins at the previous level and _____ is avoided

  vi. if workers do _____ accept lower wages, firms lay people off to cut costs and nominal spending falls _____

  vii. with _____ inflation, firms can cut costs _____ workers taking a nominal pay cut

    1. consider an inflation rate of ___% and a firm needs to cut costs by ___%

    2. assuming the firm's revenue increases with inflation, firms can _____ workers' salaries by 1% _____ cut costs by 1%

    3. _____ is avoided

2. preserves the FED's ability to _____ short-term nominal interest rates

a. suppose the real interest rate is 3%

    i. at _____% expected inflation, the nominal interest rate is

    _____%

    ii. at _____% expected inflation, the nominal interest rate is

    _____%

    iii. _____ expected inflation rates keep the FED

    _____ away from the _____ bound

b. this is particularly important in a period of _____ growth

    i. when the economy is growing _____, nominal interest

    rates are _____ because people expect lower returns on

    investment

    ii. Therefore, the FED may have difficulty _____ short-term

    rates without _____ growth

V. Deflation

    A. Good Deflation

        1. definition: when aggregate prices fall because _____

    progress reduces the cost of production, reducing prices consumers pay

    B. Bad deflation

        1. definition: when aggregate prices fall because of a fall in nominal _____

        2. problems with bad deflation

        a. when combined with _____ nominal _____

        _____, unemployment is likely (see above)

        i. definition of downward nominal wage rigidity

1. wages adjust _____ in the downward direction

b. raises debt _____ since debt for those who incurred debt

before the deflation and are now repaying the debt with more valuable

money

VI. Inflation Expectations[39]

    A. Importance

        1. the FED closely _____ inflation expectations (π_e) because inflation

expectations influence the _____ of market participants

    B. Measurement

        1. The FED monitors inflation expectations in _____ ways

            a. _____

            b. _____ measures

                i. the _____ inflation rate

                    a. the spread between _____ Treasury bonds

and Treasury Inflated Protected Security_____ of the

_____ maturity length

                        1. a _____ spread means

_____ inflation expectations

                ii. 5-year, 5-year forward inflation expectation rate

                    a. measures the _____ inflation rate over the

five-year period that begins five years from _____

        2. if inflation expectations are _____ because changes in the

---

[39] For more on inflation expectations, see here: https://www.stlouisfed.org/publications/regional-economist/april-2016/inflation-expectations-are-important-to-central-bankers-too.

aggregate price level are stable, consumption and investment decisions are stable

and long-term planning is easier, making the cost of inflation/deflation _____

Topic Thirteen: Fiscal Policy

I. Introduction

    A. What is Fiscal Policy

        1. definition

            a. when policymakers change government _____ and/or

            _____ to guide nominal spending to smooth the business

        cycle

        2. fiscal policy can be _____ or _____

            a. expansionary fiscal policy definition: when policymakers

            _____ nominal spending by increasing government spending

        and/or decreasing taxes

            b. contractionary fiscal policy definition: when policymakers

            _____ nominal spending by decreasing government spending

        and/or increasing taxes

    B. How Does Expansionary Fiscal Policy Work

        1. expansionary fiscal policy works by taking _____ resources and utilizing

        them for _____ production

            a. e.g. hiring unemployed construction workers to build a new bridge

                i. the new workers now have _____ money to spend,

                which works its way through the economy, providing spending

                _____ the initial government spending

2. under _____ employment, fiscal policy would _____ work because it would

_____ private spending

3. fiscal policy relies on _____ effects

    a. definition of multiplier effect

        i. the _____ changes in nominal spending that result

        from fiscal policy

    b. there are _____ basic multipliers related to fiscal policy

        i. fiscal _____ multiplier

        ii. lump-sum _____ multiplier

4. fiscal spending multiplier

    a. definition: the _____ by which national income changes when

    _____ spending changes

    b. In equation form: $\Delta Y = (\frac{1}{1-cy}) \Delta G_0$, where ΔY is the change in national

    income, ΔG_0 is the change in government spending, cy is the marginal

    propensity to consume, and $(\frac{1}{1-cy})$ is the fiscal spending multiplier[40]

5. lump-sum tax multiplier

    a. definition: the _____ by which national income changes when

    _____ change

    b. In equation form: $\Delta Y = (\frac{-cy}{1-cy})\Delta T_0$, where ΔY is the change in national

    income, ΔT_0 is the change in taxes, cy is the marginal propensity to

    consume, and $(\frac{-cy}{1-cy})$ is the lump-sum tax multiplier

---

[40] See appendix 2 for a formal treatment of how to derive both multipliers.

b. the lump-sum tax multiplier is _____ because a tax cut is

expansionary and a tax increase is contractionary

6. the size of each multiplier depends on the _____ propensity to

_____ (MPC)

a. definition of the marginal propensity to consume

i. the _____ of _____ income that households

_____ rather than save

b. the fiscal spending multiplier is _____ (in absolute terms) than

the lump-sum tax multiplier because consumers will _____ some of a

tax cut whereas the _____ amount of government spending is spent

C. Best Scenario for Expansionary Fiscal Policy

1. _____ emergency

2. many _____ and _____ resources

3. _____ side recession rather than a _____ side recession

II. Limits to Fiscal Policy

A. Eight Limiting Factors

1. knowledge problem

a. policymakers operate in _____ time when much of the state of the

economy is _____

i. this make it difficult for policymakers to _____

problems in the business cycle

2. timing problem

a. _____ lag

     i. policymakers take time to _____ and conditions can

     change rapidly

  b. _____ lag

     i. unused resources must be identified and dispersed _____

3. targeting problem

  a. policymakers must be able to tailor fiscal policy to the _____

  workers and sectors

     i. however, labor and capital are not _____ (i.e. not

     mutually interchangeable)

4. magnitude problem

  a. most changes in fiscal policy are not _____ compared to the size of

  the economy

     i. _____ spending is only roughly 25% of the federal

     budget

     ii. the 2020 CARES Act, which was the largest stimulus ever

     (approximately $2 trillion), was about _____ of 2020 GDP

     (which was approximately _____ trillion)

5. incentive problem

  a. policymakers face _____ incentives than firms and may act

  less efficiently when developing and implementing policy

  b. firms maximize _____

     i. these are readily seen so shareholders can _____

  c. politicians maximize _____

i. voters have a _____ memory

ii. voters are _____

6. Crowding-out

a. the _____ in _____ spending that occurs when

government increases spending

b. two possibilities

i. government borrow money, _____ interest rates,

which reduces private investment

ii. government increases _____, decreasing consumption and

investment

7. large debt changes behavior

a. debt must _____ be repaid, often through higher

_____ or future higher _____

b. if consumers and businesses perceive debt as too _____, they will

save more _____, reducing the effect of expansionary fiscal policy

8. Negative _____ shocks

1. a negative real (i.e. productivity) shock means the economy can

produce _____

2. increasing government spending will increase _____

temporarily but at the expense of long-term _____

a. monopoly board example

B. Automatic Stabilizers

1. a way to minimize lag time of fiscal policy is to use _____ stabilizers

a. definition of automatic stabilizers

      i. changes in fiscal policy _____ policymakers taking

      any _____ action

2. examples

    a. the _____ tax system

    b. _____ insurance

Topic Fourteen: Business Cycles

I. Introduction

    A. Business Cycles

      1. definition of business cycle

        a. the _____ in economic activity an economy experiences

        over _____

      2. _____

        a. definition of expansion

          i. the phase of the business cycle where the economy is growing[41]

        b. during expansion, real GDP and employment are _____

          i. the economy is utilizing _____ of its factors of production

      3. _____

        a. definition of contraction

          i. the phase of the business cycle where the economy is _____

---

[41] During expansion, the economy is moving from trough to peak. The trough is the stage of the business cycle that marks the end of economic decline. The peak is the stage of the business cycle that marks the end of economic expansion.

b. contraction is also known as a _____[42]

c. during contraction, real GDP and employment are _____

    i. the economy is _____ of its factors of production

II. Causes of Business Cycles

    A. _____ Side Shocks

        1. definition of supply side shock

            a. when output and employment changes due to changes in _____ variables

        2. real variables include factors of _____, _____, and

        _____

        3. a _____ supply shock makes the economy _____ productive,

        _____ output and employment.

            a. examples of positive supply shock

                i. computer revolution

                ii. end of Cold War

        4. a _____ supply shock makes the economy _____ productive,

        _____ output and employment.

            a. examples of negative supply shock

                i. 1970's OPEC induced oil shortage

                ii. COVID-19 government mandated shutdown

    B. _____ side shocks

        1. definition of demand side shock

---

[42] During contraction, the economy is moving from peak to trough. A recession is a significant decline in economic activity, normally visible in production, spread across the economy lasting more than a few months. See here for more detail: http://www.nber.org/cycles.html.

a. when output and employment change due to changes in nominal

_____

2. nominal spending is $Y = C + I + G + NX$

3. a _____ demand shock _____ nominal spending in the

economy, _____ output and employment, if prices are _____

    a. examples of a positive demand shock

        i. net exports rise because the world economy is improving

        ii. investment rises because businesses are more optimistic

4. a _____ demand shock _____ nominal spending in the

economy, _____ output and employment, if prices are _____

    a. examples of a negative demand shock

        i. housing crash reduces consumption

        ii. investment falls because of regulatory fear

    b. government policymakers will engage in _____ fiscal

policy, monetary policy, or both to prevent decreases in nominal spending

III. Aggregate Demand - Aggregate Supply Model

    A. Introduction

        1. definition

            a. a model showing the short-run and long-run outcomes to changes in the

economy from aggregate supply and aggregate demand _____ as

well as fiscal and monetary policy _____

    B. Aggregate Supply

        1. must distinguish between the _____ and _____ run

a. in the _____ run, prices are _____ due to market rigidities and imperfect information

    i. if prices are sticky, markets do _____ clear and there is

    _____

b. in the _____ run, prices are _____

    i. definition of flexible prices

        1. prices that adjust _____ to changes in supply and demand

    ii. if prices are flexible, markets _____

    iii. in the _____, all sticky prices become flexible

    as _____ and _____ adjust

2. long-run aggregate supply curve (LRAS)

    a. definition: a curve showing the economy's _____ growth rate when prices are flexible and unemployment is its long-run normal rate

    b. the position of the LRAS is determined by _____ factors that affect

    _____

        i. _____ of these factors depend on the rate of inflation (i.e. money neutrality holds)

    c. output can operate _____ or _____ the LRAS in the short-run

        i. if output is _____ than LRAS, constraints on capacity cause _____ pressures

            1. this happens when the unemployment rate is _____

the long-run normal rate

        ii. if output is _____ than LRAS, there is _____ in the

economy, causing _____ pressures

        1. this happens when the unemployment rate is _____

the long-run normal rate

    d. the LRAS is a vertical line

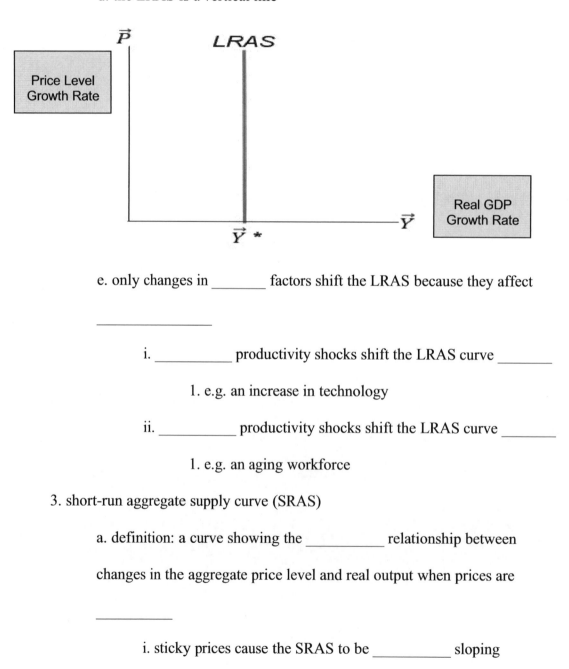

    e. only changes in _____ factors shift the LRAS because they affect

_____

        i. _____ productivity shocks shift the LRAS curve _____

        1. e.g. an increase in technology

        ii. _____ productivity shocks shift the LRAS curve _____

        1. e.g. an aging workforce

3. short-run aggregate supply curve (SRAS)

    a. definition: a curve showing the _____ relationship between

changes in the aggregate price level and real output when prices are

_____

        i. sticky prices cause the SRAS to be _____ sloping

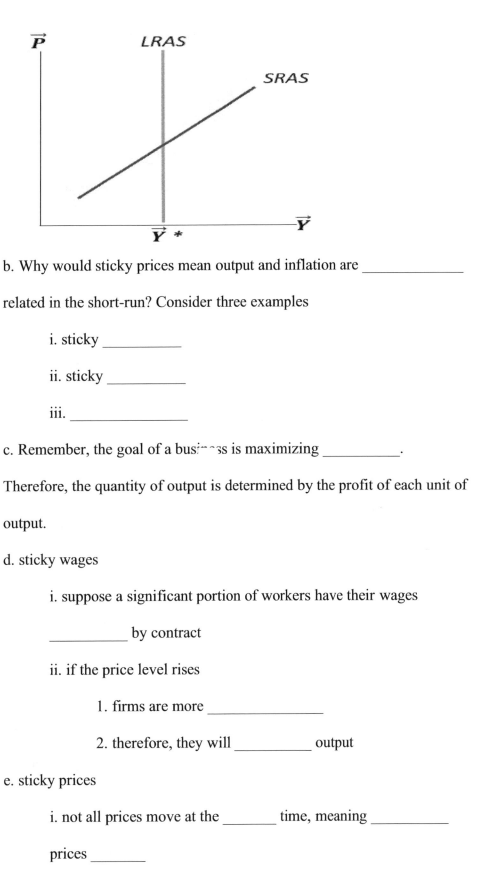

b. Why would sticky prices mean output and inflation are _____

related in the short-run? Consider three examples

    i. sticky _____

    ii. sticky _____

    iii. _____

c. Remember, the goal of a business is maximizing _____.

Therefore, the quantity of output is determined by the profit of each unit of

output.

d. sticky wages

    i. suppose a significant portion of workers have their wages

    _____ by contract

    ii. if the price level rises

        1. firms are more _____

        2. therefore, they will _____ output

e. sticky prices

    i. not all prices move at the _____ time, meaning _____

    prices _____

1. firms with relatively _____ prices see _____ demand

2. these firms _____ output

f. misperceptions

i. firms confuse changes in the _____ price level with changes in the _____ price of products they sell

1. if firms believe _____ relative price is rising from higher demand, they _____ output

g. shifts in the SRAS

i. _____ that shifts the LRAS shifts the SRAS, in the same _____, at the same _____, and by the same _____

ii. additionally

1. if inflation expectations _____, the SRAS curve shifts to the _____

2. if inflation expectations _____, the SRAS curve shifts to the _____

C. Aggregate Demand Curve (AD)

1. definition: a curve showing all the _____ of changes in the aggregate price level and real _____ growth that are consistent with a _____ growth rate of nominal spending

a. the AD curve is _____ sloping

2. building the AD curve

    a. use the Exchange Equation in growth rates

        i. $\vec{M} + \vec{V} = \vec{P} + \vec{Y}$, where $\vec{M} + \vec{V}$ is total spending

        ii. if $\vec{V} = 0\%$, $\vec{M} = 5\%$, and $\vec{Y} = 0\%$, what is $\vec{P}$?

            1. $\vec{P} =$ _____

        iii. if $\vec{V} = 0\%$, $\vec{M} = 5\%$, and $\vec{Y} = 3\%$, what is $\vec{P}$?

            1. $\vec{P} =$ _____

        iv. there are an infinite number of $\vec{P}$ and $\vec{Y}$ combinations for each level of spending

    b. since $\vec{M} + \vec{V} = \vec{P} + \vec{Y}$, _____ way to define the AD curve is all the combinations of the inflation rate and real output growth that is consistent with a specified growth rate of _____ (NGDP)

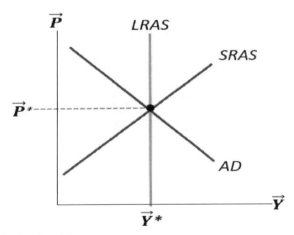

c. shifts in the AD curve

    i. AD shifts if any of the following changes

        1. growth rate of _____ (M)

        2. growth rate of _____ (V)

        3. _____ (C)

4. _____ (I)

5. _____ purchases (G)

6. _____ _____ (NX)

ii. Why? Back to the Exchange Equation

1. $\vec{M} + \vec{V} = \vec{P} + \vec{Y}$

2. total expenditures = nominal GDP, where nominal GDP

= C + I + G + NX

iii. _____ spending growth shifts the AD curve _____

1. an increase in C, I, G, NX, M, or V

iv. _____ spending growth shifts the AD curve _____

1. a decrease in C, I, G, NX, M, or V

D. Bringing the Model Together

1. first example

a. shock: nominal spending _____

i. the _____ curve shifts _____

ii. short-run equilibrium

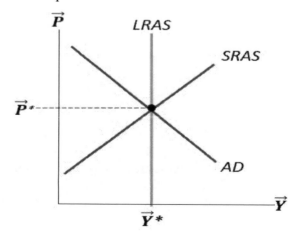

1. GDP and price level growth rates _____

b. response: _____ fiscal or monetary policy occurs

c. since output is _____ the sustainable long-run growth rate,

inflationary pressures build, _____ inflation expectations

    i. this shifts the _____ curve _____

    ii. long-run equilibrium

        1. GDP growth rate _____ back to the long-run

        rate and the price level growth rate is permanently

        _____

2. second example

    a. shock: nominal spending _____

        i. the _____ curve shifts _____

        ii. short-run equilibrium

            1. GDP and price level growth rates _____

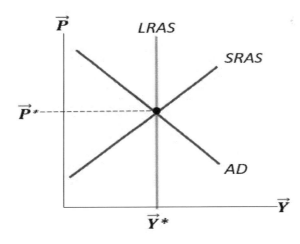

b. response: _____ fiscal or monetary policy occurs

c. since output is _____ the sustainable long-run growth rate,

deflationary pressures build, _____ inflation expectations

    i. this shifts the _____ curve _____

ii. long-run equilibrium

    1. GDP growth rate _____ back to the long-run

rate and the price level growth rate is permanently

_____

3. third example

    a. shock: nominal spending _____

        i. the _____ curve shifts _____

        ii. short-run equilibrium

            1. GDP and price level growth rates _____

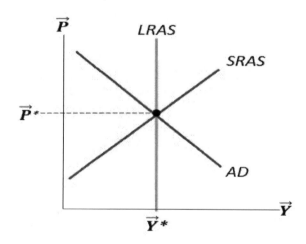

    b. response: policymakers _____ engage in _____

fiscal or monetary policy _____ inflation expectations change

        i. this shifts the AD curve to the _____

        ii. long-run equilibrium

            1. since the policy was done perfectly and timely, GDP and

price level return to their _____ growth rates

4. fourth example

    a. shock: nominal spending _____

i. the _____ curve shifts _____

ii. _____ short-run equilibrium

  1. GDP and price level growth rates _____

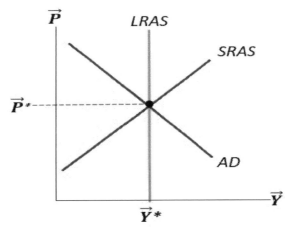

b. response: policymakers provide timely but too _____ expansionary

policy

i. this shifts the AD curve to the _____, but _____ the

original AD curve

ii. _____ short-run equilibrium

  1. GDP and the price level growth rates are _____

than the _____ equilibrium

c. since output is _____ the sustainable long-run growth rate,

inflationary pressures build, _____ inflation expectations

i. this shifts the _____ curve _____

ii. long-run equilibrium

  1. GDP _____ back to the long-run growth rate

and the price level growth rate is permanently _____

5. fifth example

    a. shock: the economy experiences a _____ productivity shock

        i. the _____ and _____ curves shift _____

    b. equilibrium

        i. GDP growth rate is _____ and the price level growth rate is

        _____

    c. Increased _____ is the best of all worlds! There is ___

reason for a policy response as the price level is falling for _____

reasons.

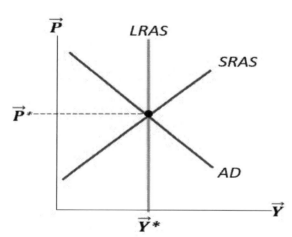

6. sixth example

    a. shock: the economy experiences a _____ productivity shock

        i. the _____ and _____ curves shift _____

    b. first equilibrium

        i. GDP growth rate is _____ and the price level growth

        rate is _____

    c. decreased productivity leads to a policy _____

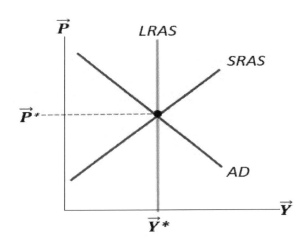

d. first possible response: policymakers pursue _____ policy

    i. the AD curve shifts _____

    ii. short-run equilibrium

        1. higher GDP _____ higher price level growth rates

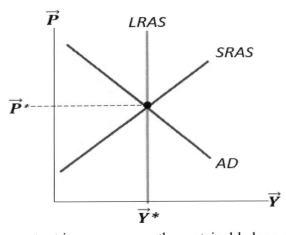

    iii. since output is _____ the sustainable long-run growth rate, inflationary pressures build, _____ inflation expectations

        1. this shifts the _____ curve _____

    iii. long-run equilibrium

        1. GDP growth rate decreases to _____ long-run rate and

the price level growth rate is _____ higher

2. the _____ is a short-run boost in GDP for

permanently higher growth rate in the price level

e. second possible response: policymakers pursue _____

policy

    i. the AD curve shifts _____

    ii. short-run equilibrium

        1. lower GDP _____ lower price level growth rates

    iii. since output is _____ the sustainable long-run growth

rate, deflationary pressures build, _____ inflation

expectations

        1. this shifts the _____ curve _____

    iii. long-run equilibrium

        1. GDP growth rate increases to _____ long-run rate and

the price level growth rate is _____ lower

        2. the _____ is a short-run reduction in GDP for

permanently lower inflation

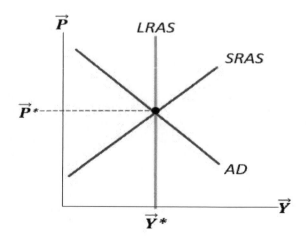

7. seventh example

a. double shock: the economy experiences a negative productivity shock

_____ nominal spending decreases

b. _____ possibilities

i. productivity shock is worse than the nominal spending shock

ii. nominal spending shock is worse than the productivity shock

c. scenario one: productivity shock is worse than the nominal spending

shock

i. LRAS, SRAS, and AD all shift _____

1. GDP growth rate is _____ and price level

growth rate is _____

ii. policymakers must _____ to pursue expansionary

policy to increase growth and the price level, contractionary policy

to decrease growth and the price level, or do nothing at all and

allow for higher growth and lower prices

iii. Negative productivity shocks _____ lead to a tradeoff.

A decrease in nominal spending makes the tradeoff _____.

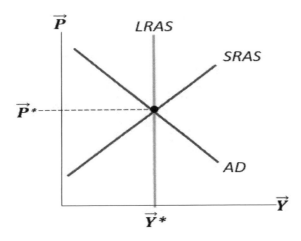

d. scenario two: nominal spending shock is worse than the productivity

shock

    i. LRAS, SRAS, and AD all shift _____

        1. GDP and price level growth rates are _____

    ii. policymakers must _____ to pursue expansionary

policy to increase growth and the price level or do nothing at all

and allow for higher growth and lower prices

    iii. doing nothing may mean the inflation rate falls _____

the inflation rate the central bank is targeting

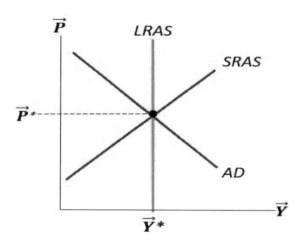

References

Griliches, Zvi. 1987. "Productivity: Measurement Problems," in *The New Palgrave: A Dictionary of* Economics, vol. 3, ed. J. Eatwell, M. Milgate, and P. Newman, 1010-13. New York: MacMillan.

Griswold, Daniel. 2011. "The Trade-Balance Creed: Debunking the Belief that Imports and Trade Deficits Are a "Drag on Growth." Center for Trade Policy Studies: Cato Institute. https://object.cato.org/sites/cato.org/files/pubs/pdf/tpa-045.pdf

Kleiner, Morris M. 2000. "Occupational Licensing." *Journal of Economic Perspectives* 14, no. 4: 189-202.

Kleiner, Morris M. and Alan B. Krueger. 2010. "The Prevalence and Effects of Occupational Licensing." *British Journal of Industrial Relations* 48, no. 4: 676-678.

Kreiner, Claus Thustrup, Daniel Reck, and Peer Ebbesen Skov. 2017."Do Lower Minimum Wages for Young Workers Raise Their Employment? Evidence from a Danish Discontinuity." *The Review of Economics and Statistics.* https://doi.org/10.1162/rest_a_00825

Landefeld, Steven J., Eugene P. Seskin, and Barbara M. Fraumeni. 2008. "Taking the Pulse of the Economy: Measuring GDP." *Journal of Economic Perspectives* 22, no. 2 (Spring): 193-216.

Lucas, Robert E. 1976. "Econometric Policy Evaluation: A Critique." Carnegie-Rochester Conference Series on Public Policy 1, 19–46.

Mishkin, Frederic S. 2007. *The Economics of Money, Banking, and Financial Markets, Eighth Edition.* New York: Pearson Education, Inc.

Mueller, Pam A., and Daniel M. Oppenheimer. 2014. "The Pen is Mightier Than the Keyboard: Advantages of Longhand Over Laptop Note Taking." *Psychological science* 25, no. 6: 1159-1168.

North, Douglass C. 1991. "Institutions." *The Journal of Economic Perspectives* 5, no. 1 (Winter): 97-112.

Yellen, Janet. 1984. "Efficiency Wage Models of Unemployment." *American Economic Review* 74, no. 2 (May): 200-250.

Appendix 1: Bond Prices and Interest Rates

Basic Definitions

A **bond** is a debt security that promises to make payments periodically for a specific time period (Mishkin 2007)

An **interest rate** (i.e. yield) is the cost of borrowing or the return to saving rental funds.

Basic Model

(1) Use a supply and demand graph, with the price of bonds on the vertical axis and the quantity of bonds on the horizontal axis.

(2) The demand for bonds is downward sloping. Why? The higher the price of bonds is, the less willing people are to purchase and own bonds (i.e. the quantity demanded for bonds falls).

(3) The supply for bonds is upward sloping. Why? The higher the price of bonds is, the more willing firms are to issue bonds (i.e. the quantity supplied for bonds rises)

(4) Where the demand and supply curves intersect, equilibrium is attained. That is, there is a price where individuals want to hold the same number of bonds that firms want to sell.

Explanation

When a bond is first sold, an equilibrium price and interest rate are set. Suppose that the general interest rate rises. Your bond is now less desirable because the bond's interest rate is lower than the interest rate on a newly issued bond. Therefore, the demand for your bond decreases. If you want to sell the bond you hold, you need to accept a lower price.

Conversely, suppose the general interest rate falls. Your bond is now more desirable because the bond's interest rate is higher than the interest rate on a newly issued bond. Therefore, the demand for your bond increases. If you want to sell the bond you hold, you can demand a higher price.

Thus, bond prices and interest rates have an inverse relationship.

Appendix 2: A Formal Treatment of the Fiscal Spending and Lump-Sum Tax Multipliers

<u>Set-up</u>
Assume we can describe the economy in the following form:

(1) $Y = C + G$
        (a) Y = national income
        (b) C = total consumption
        (c) G = total government purchases

(2) $C = c_0 + c_y Y_D$: this is the consumption function
        (a) c_0 is autonomous consumption (i.e. consumption that is independent of income)
        (b) c_y is the marginal propensity to consume
        (c) Y_D is disposable income (i.e. income after taxes)

(3) $G = G_0$
        (a) G_0 is autonomous government purchases (i.e. government purchases independent of income)

(4) $T = T_o$
        (a) T_0 is a lump sum tax (i.e. a tax that is the same for everyone and does not depend on income)

(5) $Y_D = Y - T$

<u>Solve for the Equilibrium</u>
Through substitution:

(6) $Y = c_0 + c_y(Y - T_0) + G_0$

Which can be rewritten as:

(7) $Y = c_0 + c_y Y - c_y T_0 + G_0$

Since Y is on both sides of the equation, we need to put the Y's on the same side.

(8) $Y - c_y Y = c_0 - c_y T_0 + G_0$

Which can be rewritten as:

(9) $Y(1 - c_y) = c_0 - c_y T_0 + G_0$

Solving for Y yields:

(10) $Y = (\frac{1}{1-c_y}) c_0 - c_y T_0 + G_0$

Finding the fiscal spending multiplier
Starting from the economy described in (1)

(11) $\Delta Y = \Delta C + \Delta G$, where Δ represents "change in"

This equation states that a change in national income comes from a change in consumption and a change in government purchases.

Substituting (2), (3), and (4) into (11) yields

(12) $\Delta Y = c_0 + cy(\Delta Y - T_0) + \Delta G_0$

Since autonomous consumption and the lump sum tax do not change with income, we can drop them. Therefore,

(13) $\Delta Y = cy\Delta Y + \Delta G_0$

You may ask why we did not drop G_0 since G_0 is also autonomous. Good question! When finding the fiscal spending multiplier, the variable we are changing is G_0. That is, we are considering how a change in G_0 changes total income.

Since ΔY is on both sides of the equation, we need to put the ΔY's on the same side.

(14) $\Delta Y - cy\Delta Y = \Delta G_0$

Which can be rewritten as:

(15) $\Delta Y(1 - cy) = \Delta G_0$

Solving for Y yields:

(16) $\Delta Y = (\frac{1}{1-cy}) \Delta G_0$, where $(\frac{1}{1-cy})$ is the fiscal spending multiplier

Finding the lump-sum tax multiplier
Starting from the economy described in (1)

(17) $\Delta Y = \Delta C + \Delta G$, where Δ represents "change in"

This equation states that a change in national income comes from a change in consumption and a change in government purchases.

Substituting (2), (3), and (4) into (17) yields

(18) $\Delta Y = c_0 + cy(\Delta Y - T_0) + \Delta G_0$

Which can be rewritten as:

(19) $\Delta Y = c_0 + cy\Delta Y - cyT_0 + \Delta G_0$

Since autonomous consumption and government purchases do not change with income, we can drop them. Therefore,

(20) $\Delta Y = cy\Delta Y - cy\Delta T_0$

Note that since we are changing T_0, we added the delta sign.

You may ask this time why we dropped G_0 but not T_0 this time. Again, another good question! Here we are finding the lump-sum tax multiplier. What this means is we are finding how a change in T_0 affects total income. Note that taxes directly affect the consumption function. Therefore, we keep T_0. We drop G_0 because it is autonomous (i.e. independent of income) and we are not changing it.

Since ΔY is on both sides of the equation, we need to put the ΔY's on the same side.

(21) $\Delta Y - cy\Delta Y = -cy\Delta T_0$

Which can be rewritten as:

(22) $\Delta Y(1 - cy) = -cy\Delta T_0$

Solving for Y yields:

(23) $\Delta Y = (\frac{-cy}{1-cy})\Delta T_0$, where $(\frac{-cy}{1-cy})$ is the lump-sum tax multiplier

Example

Scenario: Suppose for every dollar of extra income, the average consumer saves $0.25.

(a) Find the marginal propensity to consume.

Since the consumer saves $0.25 of every dollar of extra income, they spend $0.75 of every dollar of extra income. The marginal propensity to consume is $\frac{(\$0.75)}{(\$1.00)} = 0.75$

(b) Given the marginal propensity to consume from (a), find the fiscal spending multiplier.

The fiscal spending multiplier is: $\frac{(1)}{(1-0.75)} = 4$

(c) Given the fiscal spending multiplier from (b), find how much GDP changes if the government engages in expansionary fiscal policy and spends $200 billion.

To do this, remember from (16) that $\Delta Y = (\frac{1}{1-cy}) \Delta G_0$. *In this example,* $\Delta G_0 = \$200$ *billion and* $(\frac{1}{1-cy}) = 4$. *Therefore,* $\Delta Y = \$200$ *billion x 4* $\Rightarrow \Delta Y = \$800$ *billion*

(d) Given the fiscal spending multiplier from (b), find how much money the government spend to close an output gap of $1.6 trillion.

Here, $\Delta Y = \$1.6$ *trillion and* $(\frac{1}{1-cy}) = 4$. *Therefore,* $\$1.6$ *trillion* $= 4 \times \Delta G_0 \Rightarrow \Delta G_0 = \$400$ *billion.*

(e) Given the marginal propensity to consume from (a), find the lump-sum tax multiplier.

The lump-sum tax multiplier is: $\frac{(-0.75)}{(1-0.75)} = -3$

(f) Given the lump-sum tax multiplier from (e), find how much GDP changes if the government reduces taxes by $200 billion.

To do this, remember from (23) that $\Delta Y = (\frac{-cy}{1-cy}) \Delta T_0$. *In this example,* $\Delta T_0 = -\$200$ *billion and* $(\frac{-cy}{1-cy}) = -3$. *Therefore,* $\Delta Y = -\$200$ *billion x -3* $\Rightarrow \Delta Y = \$600$ *billion*

(g) Given the lump-sum tax multiplier from (e), find how much money the government must cut taxes by to close an output gap of $1.6 trillion.

Here, $\Delta Y = \$1.6$ *trillion and* $(\frac{-cy}{1-cy}) = -3$. *Therefore,* $\$1.6$ *trillion* $= -3 \times \Delta T_0 \Rightarrow \Delta T_0 = -\$533.33$ *billion.*

Made in the USA
Las Vegas, NV
21 August 2021

28627017R00070